Teddy Boy Blue

E. Mac M. Taylor

*Edward Taylor, in 1948, is third
from the left in the front row*

Teddy
Boy
Blue

Edward M. Taylor

Kennedy & Boyd

Kennedy & Boyd
an imprint of
Zeticula
57 St Vincent Crescent
Glasgow
G3 8NQ
Scotland

http://www.kennedyandboyd.co.uk
admin@kennedyandboyd.co.uk

First published 2008.
Reprinted 2009

Text Copyright © Edward M. Taylor 2008

Photographs © Edward M. Taylor 2008, except on pages 94, 144, (Images courtesy of The Herald & Evening Times picture archive.) and pages 170, 180, 191, 193, 234, 243, 244 (Images courtesy of The Echo, Southend)

Nutty but Nice, by Andrew Billen, is reproduced by kind permission of The Observer, copyright © Guardian News & Media Ltd 1996

ISBN-13 978 1 904999 83 6
ISBN-10   1 904999 83 2

To the other "Group of Eight" Conservative M.Ps
who joined me in being expelled for a period
from the Parliamentary Party
and who put their careers and popularity at stake,
solely because they believed
that it was wrong to surrender
more power to the European Union.
They had nothing to gain from this exercise
and a great deal to lose.

Sir Richard Body.
Nick Budgen.
Christopher Gill.
Teresa Gorman.
Tony Marlow.
Richard Shepherd.
John Wilkinson.

Acknowledgements

My grateful thanks go to the army of volunteers who helped me in every way through my Parliamentary career. Without their help and commitment I could not have done the job properly.

To give just one example, I had a weekly surgery to see constituents with problems on a Saturday morning, with between 20 and 50 callers. I needed a volunteer who would welcome the callers, have chats with them, find out sufficient details so that we could trace previous correspondence, and manage the whole business so that nobody could complain about any unfairness.

In the same way I owe a special debt to the secretaries whom I employed, who willingly worked some really crazy hours including the rush job of surgery correspondence at weekends. They never complained, and I would like them to know how much I appreciated them.

I must also mention my dear wife Sheila and the family, John, George and Louise. Far from complaining about the pressures on our lives, they seemed to thrive on it and were a constant source of support and encouragement.

Contents

Illustrations

1

Why bother to become an MP?

The one enduring memory I have, of 41 years in the House of Commons as a Member of Parliament, is that an enormous number of people are anxious to join the club. When elections take place, the candidates who have stood against me have worked night and day to further their cause, showing a devotion and intensity rarely shown in any other activity, just as I have done in my endeavours, not always successfully, to be re-elected. Even in contests for local government seats, the battle for electoral success is fierce, competitive and tough. I have seen the mildest and apparently most pleasant people work themselves into frenzies of campaigning, sometimes using tactics and ploys which they would abhor in other areas of human activity, and like other MPs I am constantly meeting eager and enthusiastic young men and women anxious to know the secrets of securing success in the battle for Parliamentary election.

The job itself has enormous drawbacks and frustrations. It is astonishingly difficult to get things done in a Parliamentary democracy. Years of campaigning can often collapse with no real achievement to show. The hours are quite appalling and even the long recesses can be hectic and harassing. Even brief holidays with the family usually end with the Member returning to a load of business that has simply piled up for attention because nobody else has the knowledge or authority to do it. The salary although much improved is not enormous, and it has been a tragedy for the good name of politics that instead of putting up the salary to as more realistic level the administration has introduced a series of allowances, some of which are simply an invitation to cheat. I am in no doubt that the majority of my former colleagues played it straight. The minority, however, are the ones who get the headlines and Members of Parliament are rarely off duty. The phone never seems to stop ringing and it is difficult to switch off. Despite this however, MPs rarely resign their seats voluntarily and the few who do, often try, rarely with success, to achieve a "come back" after a period in the world outside Westminster.

So what is the fascination of politics and what is the special attraction of being one of the people's representatives in the House of Commons? One old stager described Parliamentary careers as being like drink to an alcoholic – you do not enjoy it at the time but you miss it terribly when the withdrawal symptoms set in. I suppose that politics had a special attraction for my age group, because as a young child in the Second World War, leading politicians were little less than the saviours of our nation. When the bombs were falling in Glasgow, I can well remember the occasions when my father, who disappeared most nights on ARP duties, would announce, with hope and expectation, that Churchill would be speaking on the radio that night, and when the grand old man's deep and profound voice came over the radio waves, it was clear that he, as Prime Minister, was the person who alone was able to rally and invigorate the people to fight against the monstrous tyranny of the Germans who seemed to epitomise all that was evil in the world. It was the evil of the Germans which was cascading bombs designed to destroy our homes and kill men, women and children, and as we gathered nightly to listen to the news, the bells of Big Ben ringing out from the Houses of Parliament, seemed to indicate that this was indeed the building from which a signal and message of hope and relief from the invaders came clearly, faithfully and truthfully.

It was not just Churchill. There was a wonderful family of Commonwealth political leaders who were gladly rushing to aid Britain in its travails. When I and other children in the Netherlee Primary School were presented at school assembly with ripe red apples, which tasted sweeter than sugar, it was pointed out to us that Mr Mackenzie King, the Prime Minister of Canada, had specially asked his brave sailors to cross the dangerous waters of the Atlantic and risk death from the treacherous U-boats, just to show solidarity with the Britons in their fight for survival. I doubt if I will ever forget the unique thrill and pride of shaking hands with two rather gigantic New Zealand soldiers, who had personally engaged in mortal combat with the evil Nazis and who had come to our local church, in between their battles, to pray with our congregation for the victory of the forces of good against the forces of evil. These two warriors had come, I recall, from the other side of the world to fight for Britain, because their Prime Minister, Mr Peter Fraser, had inspired his people to help Britain and its people. Then there was Mr Jan Smuts of South Africa, who, we were told, had once disagreed with Britain, but who sunk his differences when the chips were down.

So politics for the young Taylor was not a question of Party bosses wrangling over which manifesto offered the best chance of beating inflation or bringing down unemployment. They were inspired and faultless visionaries whose qualities were unique and wonderful. The prospect of joining their ranks was clearly the kind of dream which would be the pinnacle of reasonable ambition.

I was very fortunate indeed with my home background. Certainly there was not a great deal of material prosperity, because my father, who never enjoyed good health and was racked with rheumatism, worked as a clerk in a stockbrokers' office. But certainly our family never wanted for anything and I know that a mixture of superb management of limited resources and sacrifice by my parents ensured that we did not suffer in any way. Most of all, we enjoyed the real blessing of a happy and united home.

Life was really very uncomplicated and I sometimes feel a bit guilty as an MP, now dealing with the multitude of problems facing families in distress, broken homes and financial hardship, to realise how free I was, as a child, from the dreadful unhappiness, insecurity and hardship faced by so many children today, in a world which overall is infinitely more prosperous and affluent than in the 1940s.

I think that my very first memory of life not being quite as simple and just, came with the electoral defeat of Winston Churchill in 1945 and the death of my grandfather – the first family bereavement which I experienced. In both situations I found, for the first time, that my parents did not have convincing answers.

Why did Grandpa Murray have to die? Would we really not see him again? The answer – not very convincing – was that God had somehow decided that he needed a rest. All of which did not really ring true, as the old man in a box, was dug deep into a hole in the hillside cemetery in Lamlash, where he died on holiday. Then there was Mr Churchill. "Let him finish the job", exclaimed the posters on all the billboards, and it seemed no less than justice when we had observed how Churchill alone had saved our nation. It was an election that fascinated me, and I recall, at the age of 7, spending one of the most perplexing evenings of my life, sitting through a great election rally in the Toledo Cinema. The Conservative MP, Mr Guy Lloyd, who, I was assured, was Mr Churchill's personal representative in our constituency, seemed old, crusty and rather boring. Even more perplexing was the fact that while he was indeed elected with a large majority, Mr Churchill was replaced by a rather thin and inadequate looking chap called Mr Atlee.

Why had Mr Churchill been rejected? What had gone wrong? Again the answer that God considered he needed a rest after his superhuman efforts for us all, seemed woefully inadequate, when it was abundantly clear that Mr Churchill had not requested any such rest from the Almighty and obviously questioned the merit of his spell of enforced idleness.

Looking back at these early years, I am in no doubt that the early impressions of childhood are the most lasting and enduring ones. The bonds of the Commonwealth, which were so much of our inspiration during the Second World War, shone through again in the 1950s when Britain was virtually isolated during the trauma of Suez. It is a thrilling memory for me that when the whole world seemed to be attacking Britain for a precipitate invasion of the Suez Canal and when Anthony Eden appeared to be on the verge of a physical and mental breakdown, Keith Holyoake, the Premier of New Zealand, spoke out with the firm message that our old Commonwealth ally would stick by Britain one hundred percent.

Then later when I was a very junior Minister in Ted Heath's Government, I resigned my post when Premier Heath decided to join the EEC and apparently turned his back on the Commonwealth which had always backed Britain even when it seemed wholly against their interests. It was a sad time for me, because Mr Heath had shown me great personal kindness and I also knew that to give up the job could end my Ministerial ambitions only a year after I had embarked on climbing the Parliamentary tree. However the thought of abandoning plucky and dedicated New Zealanders for a new relationship with the Continentals just did not seem tolerable or fair. It was also a difficult step to take when it was so obvious that the majority of my constituents disagreed with my decision.

However, nothing is more boring than hearing a politician engaging in self justification or explanation and so I must get back to the business of how one gets elected to Westminster – a story which still seems to offer fascination to a multitude of people.

2

How it all started

Aspiring candidates often ask for the best advice
on how to get elected to Parliament. Is it all a
question of being in the right school or club? Does
a University education help? What about articles in
the Press and media exposure? Does a glamorous
wife help? What about activity at the Party's grass
roots? How does one actually start on the journey
to Parliamentary stardom?

I must say that on the basis of my own experience
and also in light of many conversations with
colleagues, I am in no doubt that there is a huge
element of luck. There is no perfect formula for
success and some of the most able and talented
young people have struggled for years, doing all
the "right things" and never succeeding. However
there are certain basic rules that I think are worth
pursuing. The first essential ingredient is a desire to
get things done through politics. Unless there is a
real commitment to seek a place in politics, as a tool
to achievement of policies, it is difficult to maintain
enthusiasm for the task on hand in difficult and
depressing times.

The second ingredient is to find out how the
political system works. Unless you can establish the
actual mechanism for candidate selection in the
various parties, it is almost impossible to achieve
success. There is little point in having the very best
of friendships and connections in the upper tiers
of political activity unless you also get to know the
grass roots people who decide who is going to be
chosen to stand as a party candidate. I think the
third ingredient, is a willingness to participate in

local government. Local government is an essential part of our democracy and quite apart from the educative bonus of taking part in the business of government at a local level, there is no doubt that councillors tend to be deeply enmeshed in constituency politics.

Councillors depend on local organisations for their election and it is remarkable just how many of the present MPs in Parliament have at some time been local councillors. However even if these ground rules are followed to the letter, luck is still the determining force. Being available at the right time, in the right place is the real key to success and there is just no way in which this can be planned out.

I entered representative democracy as a candidate in a rather unusual way. Most of my schooldays – from the age of 6 until 16 – were spent at the High School of Glasgow.

The school has long since been abolished in its previous form and survives only as a private school which has taken over the name of what was an historic old school in the centre of Glasgow. It was a kind of grammar school run by the Corporation of Glasgow and had minimal fees – about £6 per term when I joined – and there was a selection test for entry. Pupils at the age of 5 were subjected to an intelligence test and normally there were about ten applicants for every place.

The debates on aptitude tests for the very young became a live political issue when later I was briefly the Scottish Education Minister and I had to listen to long speeches and receive deputations from educationalists and others who maintained that it was impossible to establish a pupil's educational potential with a test at 11 years of age. I therefore commissioned a study by officials on the actual educational attainments of those who were subject to a test at age 5 and it was astonishing to see that about 90 per cent of those selected at this very young age were successful in obtaining university entrance qualifications. This led me to the conclusion that while some argued that the basis of educational success was environmental or hereditary, the real key was parental expectation. This view was confirmed later on when we had the development of neighbourhood comprehensives. In some giant comprehensives, the norm was, that if your child achieved some "O" levels, he was doing quite well. In others, the norm was that if the child did not reach college or university, he or she had not done well. The clear evidence was that actual educational attainment tended to be influenced in general by the accepted parental expectations in the community or school. For this reason, my view has always been that through the territorial comprehensive system in cities, there was a development of virtual class segregation in education. The survival of the grammar schools, by comparison, gave able youngsters from working class homes an infinitely better chance of achievement than if they were condemned to education in a neighbourhood school where there were lower norms of achievement.

My stay at the High School was a happy one. There was a wide social mix in the school and we were particularly fortunate in the quality of teaching staff, but did these centres of excellence survive on the backs of condemning those not selected to inferior education? I think that the old junior secondaries or secondary moderns have never been given the credit they deserved. In my view, the basis of happiness and success in education is achievement and the old secondary moderns did provide the less gifted children with an opportunity to succeed when they might otherwise have been "lost" in a comprehensive with mixed attainments and abilities. Someone had to be captain and many had to be prefects in the secondary moderns. There were prizes and awards for those who were top in the various exams and I believe passionately that we lost a great deal when the secondary moderns disappeared without a word of regret from the educationalists.

At school, my only commitment to politics was being Secretary of our Debating Association. This was a club, which met after school hours, and was not much supported by pupils. However, I think that the one small service I performed was to make the society more topical and controversial, which led to crowded and fiery debates. One of the most respected and time honoured institutions in the school was the cadet corps – a kind of school army – with pupils in uniform marching up and down twice a week in the playground and engaging in map reading and military exercises from time to time in the scout estate near Glasgow. I can recall creating quite a stir in the school by initiating a debate with the Motion "That in view of recent disclosures about the Atom Bomb, the school corps is now obsolete and should be disbanded". Our school corps sergeant major packed many of his cadets into the debate, but after the most fiery discussion in which I and my supporters were virtually accused of being the then equivalents of the Greenham Common protestors, the Motion was passed by a handful of votes.

The only other political activity I can recall was organising a massive petition of pupils, which I presented with trepidation to the headmaster – called the Rector. The High School had a long tradition of being a rugby playing school, which seemed to me to be unjust because most of the pupils would have preferred football. Hampden Park, the scene of the great Scottish English football matches and Ibrox and Celtic Park – homes of the Glasgow Rangers and Celtic Football Clubs, were an integral part of Glasgow life. So I organised a giant petition of the pupils calling for the abolition of rugby and the substitution of football. Sadly my experiment in democracy was a disaster because the Rector – in a cold and unfriendly manner I did not associate with him – advised me sternly that the school was not a democracy and that I had better concentrate on my studies and abandon my dissident and revolutionary activities.

Academically, school was successful for me and after leaving the buildings I proceeded to Glasgow University. It was not a conscious decision because it never really struck me that there was any alternative course. Nor, strange to say, did it ever seem a possibility that I would go to any other university apart from Glasgow. Nowadays, students seem to look round the UK for a university place and seem to prefer one well away from home, but in Glasgow in the early 1950s, the normal pattern was for pupils to leave school and go to their home university. Not only did this make the transfer less disturbing for young people, but the form of university education was not all that different from school.

My first year subjects were history, english and maths and the tuition was largely similar to school. We went to lectures, which lasted for an hour instead of the school 40 minute period. The classes tended to be about 150 in number as opposed to the school's 35 or so. The basic difference was that we had to submit many essays instead of the school's homework. Another difference was that instead of marks we were awarded Greek symbols as merit awards for essays. A roll of pupils was held to ensure that attendance was kept and without a good attendance record, a "class ticket" was not awarded and the ticket was a necessary item if the exams were to be sat.

It was only in the later years when we took Honours subjects that there were tutorial group discussions with lecturers. In short, university was very much like an extension of school. The only real difference was the time that we spent in the University Union – a magnificent building where students had their meals and where, at lunchtime and in the evenings, there were multitudes of meetings and discussions. All the political parties held meetings and all the great topics of the day were ventilated in packed meetings in the great debating hall.

What made the university probably the best training ground for potential politicians was that about eight times a year there were major debates which started at 1pm and went on till about 10pm.

Students were required to sit in party benches for these debates, which followed the normal Parliamentary form. The student magazines gave thorough and comprehensive reports of the debates giving assessments of the debating prowess of the participants. All the Parties had their own benches – Conservative, Labour, Liberal, Scottish Nationalist, the Distributist (a rather unusual party committed to giving every citizen three acres and a cow but which largely consisted of students from the Roman Catholic state schools), the Communists and the Independents. There was also a bench for the Socialist Unity Party, which was, at the time, a kind of Bennite group, somewhere between the Socialists and Communists. Students simply sat in the Party benches they preferred and there was the opportunity, if they wished, to change parties from debate to debate. The debates tended to be tough and argumentative and were probably more political and less tepid and flowery because the Union was a Men only one. The ladies had their own Union where debates were also held.

This rather unique form of Parliamentary debating gave students the opportunity of speaking and dealing with interventions and heckling and there was always plenty of fire and passion. Students followed Parliamentary procedures to the last detail and everyone had a constituency (of their choice) and had to refer to other students by their constituency and not their names.

I sat on the Conservative benches, largely, I believe, because it seemed the respectable thing to do and not because, at the time, I had any great knowledge of the details of party policies. In addition, to be frank, I think that my parents might have been distressed if I had associated myself with any other political group.

However, I must admit that I was not one of the kings of the Union debates. Several times I found that the policies being put forward by the Party "leadership" did not make a great deal of sense and after a while I took to speaking from the Independent benches. While the University magazines always gave reasonably favourable reports of my speeches (perhaps the reason being, that the writer in the student Press was a friend called Bill Rankin, who became Features Editor of the News of the World), I think that at best I was regarded as an interesting, but not very inspiring maverick.

There were several "giants" in the Tory Party at the time who seemed destined for a political career, but none actually made the grade, and I have a feeling that if I had aspired to become one of the

Party hierarchy who had the honour of delivering the key "wind up" speeches to packed debating halls, I might never have got involved in politics at all.

What created the opportunity initially for me, was one of these chance encounters, which are often the key to political success. After a meeting of a local party branch, which I attended intermittently, but without any real commitment, I was talking to a rather rotund and cheery chap whose name I did not know and deploring something that had happened at the University debate. My complaint was that I had not been called upon to speak. "Why don't you come along to the GPDA? You can always make a speech there". This is how I think it all started for me.

The cheery chap was called Jimmy Henderson and the GPDA was a rather unique body called the Glasgow Parliamentary Debating Association. It was a body of political enthusiasts that, for about 100 years, had met together each Thursday evening to play at Parliaments. It was a relatively small body – with about 40 regular attendees – and they simply met each week to enjoy the pleasure of having a debate. It was the "real thing". There was a speaker - a wonderful, kindly old councillor called Alex Hart - a Prime Minister and a small Cabinet. There was a Question Time before debates and then a debate either on a Bill or an opposition Motion.

Many of the members were elderly but they covered the whole age range, and it was great fun. Perhaps the jolliest part of the evening was when an unfortunate Minister had to answer questions. The Minister had no advance warning of the questions. He did not have any civil service back up, and often he was asked things which he had no knowledge of whatsoever, but the whole procedure not only enabled any person interested in politics to talk about the issues of the day it was also small enough for the members to get to know each other as friends and colleagues.

I had some great times at the GPDA and made several speeches on the topics of the day.

There were several Glasgow councillors in the GPDA. Glasgow politics, then, were going through a period of change. There were two main parties. Firstly there was Labour, and opposing them was a party called the Glasgow Progressive Party. Most of its members were Conservatives, but the Party maintained its independence in dealing with Conservative Governments in Whitehall and St. Andrews House. To be fair, there were also many Progressive members who claimed that they would not wish to be linked to the Conservative Party and others who insisted that politics had no place in local government. It was actually a recipe for success because after the Conservatives moved into local government, the non-socialist membership of the Glasgow Council faded away to about nothing. At present there is only one Conservative Councillor in the Glasgow city council while there used to be a strong army of Progressive councillors. Apart from this, the procedure freed local Conservative Parties from the substantial financial cost of paying for local government elections.

I was just 20 when my first political opportunity hit me. Alex Hutton, a councillor representing my own Cathcart Ward where I lived, and one of the powerful firebrands of the GPDA, spoke to me after one of the debates and put the proposition which shook me. "How about being a ghost candidate, Ted? You just sign this paper – that is all you have to do". And this was how it all started for me. If Alex had not handed me that paper, I doubt if I would ever have contemplated representative politics – or had the opportunity.

3

My first campaign

The form I was handed seemed to be very complicated. First, the paper had a space for the ward which the candidate wished to stand for, as a candidate. Second, there was a space for a proposer and seconder. Next, there was a space for a number of electors, who had to support the candidature. Finally, there was a space for a signature by a Justice of the Peace, who was required to be present to testify to all the signatures.

So it all seemed to be very complicated.

The obvious questions I had were, which ward I was being considered for, how on earth I would find people to support my candidature and how I was expected to run a campaign, prepare speeches for meetings and organise a team of helpers to hand round my pamphlets. Perhaps most important of all, was the fact that I had not the slightest idea of the policies of the Progressive Party and how I could put this across.

These worries, I was assured, were quite unnecessary. The form would be "seen" to, so long as I signed it. It was not possible to say for which ward I was to stand as a candidate until four weeks before Polling Day. I was, it was emphasised, to be a "ghost candidate", which meant simply that the voters in a "hopeless" ward would be given an opportunity to vote for a candidate for the Progressive Party. There would therefore be no need for me to do anything at all – unless I wished to do so, but it was emphasised that any such campaigning would be pointless because the seat would be a hopeless one – that is one which the Progressive Party could not hope to win, even in its wildest dreams.

I was naturally terrified by the whole business. Would I be in some way doing something wrong in standing as a candidate without any campaign? I could well remember all the warnings about the dangers of signing papers. So I hastily explained that I was in a hurry and would "think about it". However, on returning home, my parents quickly sorted me out and explained that it was really quite an honour to be asked to stand for the Council, and Jimmy Henderson assured me that if I had any problems, he would sort them out.

So the following Thursday, I told Councillor Hutton that the deal was on, and I signed the paper. When I started talking about pamphlets and meetings, Alex immediately counselled caution. "You haven't an earthly in the kind of seat we'll give you, Ted. Perhaps it would be best not to tell you which ward you are standing for!" he exclaimed, and in a fit of anxiety he urged me not to allow the election business to interfere with my studies at university. It was sound advice, because the election was in May and my exams were in June.

However, I went home that night, full of excitement. Where would the ward be? Was there not the remotest chance that I might win the election? There had been all kinds of upsets in the past and it was certainly difficult to concentrate on my studies.

The biggest piece of "one-upmanship" which I enjoyed that week was when one of the leaders of the Conservative Party in the University, asked me – in terms which conveyed that I was being granted a major favour – if I would be available to join the election team to assist the Progressive candidate standing in the Progressive held Hillhead Ward.

"Sorry", I replied, with a disdain which I always felt ashamed of to this day – "I am standing as

a Progressive candidate myself for the election!"
The look of astonishment on the face of our
Party's Mr Big was remarkable, and for the rest
of the week, I had a whole series of enquiries
from the disbelieving students about whether
I was really standing as a candidate and how it
had all happened. I feel that they considered that
there was something not quite right about the
whole business, because I was one of the lesser
fry in the Party at University and not considered
to be in any way amongst the most talented or
loyal. So I had my few days of glory, waiting with
trepidation to hear about where I was standing.
Of course the feeling of blind panic came on.
Would the Party not have a vacancy at all and
how on earth would I prevent myself becoming
the laughing stock of the University Conservative
Club? If it all fell through I thought that I would
have to abandon any interest in politics and keep
a very low profile indeed.

But then the joyful day came, with a letter through
the letterbox about four weeks before Polling Day.
It was a letter from the Secretary of the Progressive
Party expressing satisfaction with the fact that I had
been selected as candidate for the Townhead Ward,
that I should attend a meeting of Party candidates
the following Saturday and that my Election
Headquarters were to be at the Glasgow Central
Conservative Rooms, where the Agent would be
glad to assist in my campaign.

My first task was obviously to find out where
Townhead actually was. I knew that it was in the
City Centre, but had no idea where the boundaries
would be. Certainly my feeling was that it was the
kind of area where supporters of the Rightist cause
would be few and far between.

However, as it was Friday, my first task was to attend the candidates meeting and this was one of the most exciting days of my life.

I was immediately given a warm welcome by the Candidates' Convener, Councillor Walter Miller, who introduced me to a whole series of councillors who were obviously very important and significant characters.

Then we had the campaign strategy to set out.

A pamphlet outlining on one side, the party's policies would be provided entirely free of charge and the candidates themselves could print their own personal message and details of public meetings on the other side. Happily one of the councillors, Jimmy Thomson, was a printer and so he could do everything for us.

A substantial campaign fund was available for the contest as a result of the hard work of the fund-raisers and allocations were being made, varying from £250 in the key marginal seats, down to £20 for the poor seats. Townhead, for no apparent reason, was allocated £25. However the candidates were advised that if at all possible they should not spend the entire allocation.

The aim was to wrest control of the City from the Labour Party and all the signs were apparently very good indeed. Councillor Gordon Reid, the leader of the Group, gave a special message of hope and assured the candidates in the "more difficult Wards", that they had a special role to play in fighting as hard as they could to ensure that the Labour Party activists were pinned down in their own seats and thus unable to concentrate their forces on the key marginals.

The campaign theme was to be that rates were too high and that the Progressives would reduce them, and a whole series of examples of Labour spending scandals were given, which we were to use as a means of persuading people that such scandals would not occur if the prudent Progressives, with their sound business experience, were to be in charge of the City's affairs.

We were also told that council house rents were too low and should be increased – a proposal which evinced a rather horrified response from candidates standing in seats which consisted largely of council houses. But this, it seems, was no problem because the campaigns, we were assured, had to be tailored to the needs of each ward.

We were also told to check up on our nomination papers and get them completed by our local offices. So the paper that I had signed, on the basis that there was no problem at all, was handed back to me.

It was all very exciting and hopeful.

On Monday, instead of attending my history lecture, I made my way to the Townhead Conservative Office. It was a rather gloomy and forbidding place known locally as the coffin hall because it consisted of a small office and a larger hall shaped exactly like a coffin. I knocked warily at the door and when it opened I met the delightful Organising Secretary. I introduced myself as the Progressive candidate for Townhead and then sat down to discuss the campaign strategy.

"Are you going to have a campaign?" was the first question, clearly asked more in hope than expectation. Poor Mrs Helen McGregor had for years been given the task of promoting Conservatism in Glasgow Central which was a similar task to selling ice-cream to Eskimos and each year she had a similar task of organising elections for "ghost candidates" who never actually did any campaigning. The

Association's membership was at a very low ebb indeed and it seemed that the Rooms were only kept going by renting out the coffin hall for wedding receptions, pensioners meetings and gatherings of the local Orange Lodge. It was a depressing business. Seeing the look of longing in her friendly and hopeful face, I could not bring myself to say that I was yet another "ghost" and so explained in a spirit of bravado that I indeed intended to conduct a vigorous campaign.

"You mean that you will be putting pamphlets round the doors?"

"Of course", I replied.

"And will you hold a meeting?"

Gulping with anxiety I replied that this was indeed my intention. It was as though I had rewarded dear Mrs McGregor with the news that she was being invited to tea at Buckingham Palace. Within minutes we were getting down to the task of writing out my side of the pamphlet and arrangements were also made to meet the campaign team.

The campaign team met that night. It wasn't exactly the kind of army which would strike fear into Napoleon's army. In fact it consisted entirely, apart from the old lady whose name I cannot recall, of a wonderful old dedicated Tory called Mrs Irvine, her daughter Renee and her grandchildren, Ann and Tommy, but what they lacked in numbers they made up for in enthusiasm. This tiny family group had, it emerged, the ability to run up and down all the stairs of Townhead putting pamphlets through all the doors. And so we got down to work. The budget of £25 was rather limited, but this enabled us to buy 2,000 pamphlets and to order 10 posters.

What about the posters? We racked our brains for a campaign slogan and eventually emerged with the dynamic answer:- "Teddy Taylor for Townhead!"

1950 - 15/4

1954 - £1 - 0 - 4

1957 - £1 - 4 - 2

NOW - £1 - 6 - 8

Recognise these? These are Glasgow's Rates.

The Progressive Party believe Your Rates could be cut by—

1. A drive for economy.

2. An ending of the unjust system where tenants and owners of private property subsidise all tenants of municipal houses irrespecive of financial needs.

3. A speedy reorganisation of Glasgow's Transport.

4. An injection of private and business enterprise into municipal policy.

Published by H. McGREGOR, Election Agent, 24 Monkland St.
Printed by THE ALBION PRINTING Co., 13 Dundas St.

1958, June

TOWNHEAD MUNICIPAL ELECTION
1958

—————————

Dear Elector,

   As Progressive candidate for this Ward, I invite your support and vote on Polling Day,

Tuesday, 6th May, 1958

Yours faithfully,

Teddy Taylor.

1958, June

And so the battle commenced. My opponent was a tough little lady called Councillor Mrs Isa Carter. I met her on a number of occasions during the campaign and it was clear that she regarded me with the gravest of suspicion. Her main topic of conversation was that the Progressives had a cheek seeking to get votes in Townhead at all, but it obviously unnerved her a little to have somebody standing against her who was prepared to put out some pamphlets.

Elections South of the Border seem to consist largely of canvassing, but in Glasgow Council Elections there was no need for the candidates to have any direct contact with the voters at all. It was simply a question of putting pamphlets through letterboxes. Then there was the meeting. We advertised it in the pamphlet and I can recall that it was the most worrying part of the whole campaign.

The friendly Councillor Miller had kindly agreed to act as Chairman, but what was not clear was how to make a speech and how I would deal with all the heckling and questions which, I had been warned, would inevitably arise.

I need not have worried too much, because the audience consisted of Mrs Irvine, Renee, Tommy, Ann, my parents and the husband and sister-in-law of the agent.

It all went rather nicely. Councillor Miller gave a splendid introduction saying what a wonderful candidate I was, how lucky Townhead was to have me as their candidate and suggesting that Mrs Isa Carter was going to get a run for her money. I then gave a little speech pointing out some of the scandalous examples of Labour's excessive spending in Glasgow and pointed out that things would be much better for everyone if the Progressives were to manage Glasgow with the principles of sound business. Poor Tommy and Ann looked a bit bored with the whole proceedings, but everyone present clapped furiously and Walter Miller, in his most kindly way said that he had been privileged to hear such a splendid account of the City's problems and solutions.

As Polling Day came nearer, the excitement increased. Renee and Ann came back with reports of people who had said that they were going to vote for me. When Polling Day actually arrived, the Party's loudspeaker van came for an hour and I had the delightful experience of announcing to the bemused shoppers in Townhead that they should vote for Teddy Taylor for Townhead.

We then all proceeded to the Count. It was a really exciting time because all the votes for all the wards in Glasgow were counted in the giant Kelvin Hall. The Party bosses wandered round all the tables looking for signs of the great Progressive uplift and there were shouts of great glee from the assembled Party workers as the results were announced over the loudspeaker. The greatest thrill for me was to see the ballot papers in which a cross had been placed against my name. It seemed almost incredible that Townhead residents had taken the trouble to go round to the local schools on a cold day for the sole purpose of voting for me.

The result was predictable. I got about 800 votes. Mrs Carter received about 1,700. She made a comradely little speech thanking Townhead for staying loyal to Labour and she expressed the hope that I would stand again in a seat where there were better prospects for my Party. I gave a silly little speech congratulating her on her success but warning her that the tide of Progressive thought was sweeping through Townhead and would eventually result in our triumph. Mrs Carter gave a rather undignified guffaw. Walter Miller came rushing round to assure me that according to some complex calculations, I had achieved some kind of swing.

The next day came the feeling of anti-climax.

The local papers didn't seem to think that anything of great significance had happened in Townhead, reserving their comments for the Labour gains that had been made.

And so it was all over. Poor Ann had been in tears at the Count and old Mrs Irvine said with determination that we would win Townhead some day. I doubt if any candidate has ever had such wholly dedicated workers as the Irvine family and I felt that somehow I had let them down. However the next week it was back to study at University and the more mundane things of life.

It seemed at least for the present, my political career had come to a halt.

4

Pre-election battles

The Townhead campaign, which in no sense entered the political record books, looked like being the end of my political career for some time and I thought that I would just have to wait until 1959 to see if the Party would want me to stand again in some wasteland ward. However, I kept the link with Glasgow Central and Mrs Helen McGregor.

We actually founded a group called the Townhead Young Conservatives and captured the imagination of the youthful members of the community by holding a free dance in the coffin hall. It was not exactly a rave up. There were no discos at that time and in place of the jazz band I had been hoping for, the music was provided by the infinitely cheaper group which consisted of a plump and unshaven character with an accordion and a very thin old age pensioner who tapped a drum in approximate time with the accordion. There was a lavish buffet consisting of large bottles of lemonade and digestive biscuits. Mrs McGregor somehow found the funds to finance the event and during the interval when the bandsmen disappeared, I was invited to make a dramatic appeal to the assembled company of ten rather shy and giggly girls and six embarrassed and disinterested senior schoolboys whom Mrs McGregor had somehow gathered together with her contacts.

I explained to them again that the Labour Council in Glasgow was wasting ratepayers money hugely on things like running farms and sending councillors on free trips to America and appealed to them all to join the Townhead Young Conservatives so that we could lead a crusade together for justice and financial prudence. This could be done by signing their names and addresses on a piece of paper on the buffet table which had already been made rather sodden with lemonade spilt all over it.

There was then a rather embarrassed silence and the whole evening seemed to fizzle out because the two bandsmen just never reappeared. They had apparently gone to a local pub for refreshment and must have met up with more exciting company than the Townhead Young Conservatives.

It really didn't make all that much difference because nobody had actually danced at all. My dancing prowess was limited to waltzes and quicksteps and the accordion expert's music just didn't seem appropriate to either of these dances.

However, as the company departed we saw that five names and addresses were on the paper and so Mrs McGregor wrote to them all inviting them to a meeting the following week.

When the five gathered I explained that I was the Chairman of the Townhead Young Conservatives and that they were the Committee. We then got down to writing out a programme but the only suggestion was one from me that we should have Councillor Miller as a speaker and Mrs McGregor suggested a Beetle Drive.

However the step had been taken, Mrs McGregor was able to tell our Party headquarters that the Central Division had its own Young Conservatives and from that moment I started getting invitations to all kinds of political gatherings in my capacity as Chairman of the Branch.

It was rather difficult to keep the momentum going. Councillor Miller did indeed come along to speak to us and assured us that the future of our

City rested on young people like ourselves. The Beetle Drive took place although the numbers had to be boosted by some elderly pensioners who came along at Mrs McGregor's request. This was all rather embarrassing because that evening we had a surprise visit from the area boss of the Conservative Party – the delightful Andrew Strang, who later was to head the Scottish Conservative Association and who had clearly been impelled to come and see for himself the fantastic Tory revival in Townhead. There were four very elderly pensioners – who were clearly not of YC age, three of our Committee and me. It was clear at the outset that we had the greatest difficulty understanding the rules of Beetle far less the overthrow of the Labour stronghold on Glasgow. However, despite my embarrassment, Andrew seemed to be very pleased and positive and Mrs McGregor was clearly as pleased as punch.

The breakthrough however, came again, by accident.

A Labour councillor died. He had represented the Cowlairs Ward – part of the Socialist Springburn stronghold and Cowlairs was the "downmarket" part of that rather sad old part of Glasgow built round the giant North British locomotive works. NB had specialised in building steam engines – some of which can still be seen in remote parts of Africa and Pakistan.

The consensus of opinion in the Progressive Party was that there was little point in fighting the by-election because the seat was plainly impossible and funds for campaigning were scarce. However, it seemed that the hawks in the Party led a revolt and insisted that we had to harry the Socialists at every opportunity and they carried a vote in the Group meeting to insist that the by-election be contested.

So Gordon Reid, the Party leader, had the task of finding a candidate in a hurry to fight a by-election in the month of December.

No doubt he tried a number of possibilities, but clearly at some stage he remembered me. The reason was that at an early part of the Townhead campaign I had explained that I could not attend a pre-election candidates meeting because it was my 21ˢ birthday. This caused alarm in the ranks because it had been assumed that I was over 21 and therefore eligible to stand as a candidate. There was a bit of a flap, which caused me to have to go with Councillor Reid to see the Town Clerk to explain the problem. Happily it emerged that there was no problem, because I was on the voters roll and my birthday on 18th April allowed me to fit in with the rules.

So I had a phone call from Councillor Reid asking if I would take on the Party's cause in the Cowlairs by-election. By this time I had graduated and was working on the Commercial Editorial Staff of the Glasgow Herald. Although the work was not directly related to assessing economic strategy, but to taking down over the phone details of the fish prices secured at various ports and writing them out for publication, it was clear my time was limited. However, one of my best friends, Eric Abell, who had a year off because of an exam failure in his medical degree, kindly agreed to be my campaign mastermind and I had the benefit of being available in the mornings myself because the hours of work were 3pm to 9pm. I also had to get the permission of my boss – John Sherret – and he could not have been more kind. I think that I had made a bit of a name for myself in the paper for the simple reason that I had turned up on my first day at work with a bowler hat and umbrella. This seemed appropriate

GLASGOW MUNICIPAL BY-ELECTION 1958

Tuesday, 9th December
(COWLAIRS WARD)

THE PROGRESSIVE CANDIDATE
EDWARD M. TAYLOR
M.A.

TO THE ELECTORS OF COWLAIRS WARD

Dear Elector,

I write to you as the Progressive Party candidate for your Ward at the forthcoming By-Election and invite your vote and active support.

You must be aware of the irresponsibility and folly with which the Labour Town Council has managed our City's affairs since it gained power—the ever-increasing burden of Rates is surely adequate proof of Labour's unbusinesslike and spendthrift administration. **Rates at £1 8s. 1d. this year, compared with only 15s. 4d. in 1950 when my party was in power, must be considered excessive when we consider the quality of the services we receive in return.**

The unjust system whereby, at present, tenants and house owners pay not only for their own houses but also a large part of the rents of Council house tenants, is all too representative of Socialist injustice. In Townhead, where I was a candidate in May, I met many people, especially Pensioners, who found great difficulty in paying their own rent and complained bitterly about having to subsidise Council house tenants in far better circumstances than themselves. **A Progressive administration would put an end to this injustice but would introduce a rebate scheme for Council house tenants who could not afford to pay more.**

In conclusion, if you show your confidence in me and in my party by electing me on **9th December,** I promise that I will do all in my power to attend to your problems as well as those of Glasgow.

Yours sincerely,

EDWARD M. TAYLOR.

1958, September

33

**Letter to the Electors of Cowlairs Ward
from the Chairman of the Progressive Group in Glasgow Town Council.**

_____

I am writing to you as Chairman of the Progressive Group in Glasgow Town Council to ask you to vote for Mr. Edward Taylor at the By-Election in Cowlairs Ward on 9th December.

I commend Mr. Taylor to you as a man who would make an excellent Town Councillor and Local Representative. He appreciates the problems arising in Cowlairs Ward and will give personal attention to all matters brought to his notice.

One of the main problems confronting the Town Council in recent years has been the question of Municipal House Rents. The Progressive Group has realised for a long time that some sort of review would have to take place and have at recent elections placed this belief fairly and squarely before the Ratepayers. It was not a popular electioneering point in certain Wards but the Progressive Group have undertaken to govern the City in the best interests of ALL irrespective of class, creed or party, and it was in furtherance of this undertaking that they insisted, election after election, that a review of Corporation House Rents was necessary to restrain the ever-increasing Housing deficiency which was contributing so substantially to the present high rates of 28s. 1d. in the £. A great injustice was being done in many Wards of the City, such as Cowlairs, where the people were subsidising Corporation house tenants to a far greater degree than was fair, looking to the fact that in many cases the Corporation tenants were living in better circumstances and were in receipt of larger incomes than those who were called upon to meet the heavy deficit.

The pursuance of that policy is proof of honesty of purpose. It certainly meant that we lost the chance of a popular vote with the result that we have found it hard to maintain our present voting strength in the Corporation.

At the moment the Town Council is reviewing Corporation House Rents but you can be assured that the Progressive Group are watching the position very closely to see that any increases decided upon will be accompanied by a rebate scheme for those who may not be able to afford to pay a more reasonable rent, and they will watch carefully that no social injustice shall be done.

I have s poken to you frankly in this letter. I wanted to do so and I felt that you would wish me to do so. I earnestly trust that you will vote for Mr. Taylor as Progressive Councillor at this By-Election.

Yours sincerely,

W. GORDON REID.

1958, September

34

VOTE FOR PROGRESS—VOTE PROGRESSIVE

Vote TEDDY TAYLOR for Cowlairs

TAYLOR CARES FOR COWLAIRS

Glasgow citizens are paying more than ever before for education through the City rates, but are the children being educated any better ? A Progressive Corporation would see that Glasgow got value for every penny spent.

ABOUT YOUR CANDIDATE

Mr. Taylor is at present employed in the Commercial Editorial staff of a leading Glasgow newspaper.

He was educated in a Glasgow School and at Glasgow University where he studied Economics and Politics and graduated with Honours.

He is most interested in public affairs and is the Vice-Chairman of Glasgow (Central) Young Unionists. Apart from Politics his main interests are youth organisations, music and reading.

Glasgow's transport was once admired throughout Europe. What do you think of it now ? Vote Progressive for a new and better policy.

FOR SOUND ADMINISTRATION VOTE PROGRESSIVE VOTE FOR

TEDDY TAYLOR

1950—15/4

1954—£1 0s. 4d.

1957—£1 4s. 2d.

1958—£1 8s. 1d.

Recognise these figures ? They are Glasgow's Rates.

THE PROGRESSIVE PARTY BELIEVES THAT YOUR RATES COULD BE CUT BY—

(A) **A Drive for Economy.**

(B) **An ending of the unjust system whereby tenants and owners of private houses subsidise all tenants of Council houses whether they can afford to pay more or not.**

(C) **A speedy reorganisation of Glasgow's Transport.**

(D) **An injection of private and business enterprise into Municipal Policy.**

1958, September

WEDNESDAY, 3rd DECEMBER, 1958

St. Roch's Junior Secondary School,
Royston Road

THURSDAY, 4th DECEMBER, 1958

Petershill Junior Secondary School,
Petershill Road

MONDAY, 8th DECEMBER, 1958

Springburn School,
Gourlay Street

All Meetings at 8 p.m.

WHERE TO HEAR

WHERE TO HELP
& Obtain Help

COMMITTEE ROOMS

Unionist Rooms, Atlas Street

HOW TO VOTE

Support the PROGRESSIVE

Candidate on

TUESDAY, 9th DECEMBER

VOTE THUS:

| TAYLOR, EDWARD M. | X |

Printed by C. L. WRIGHT LTD., 100 West George Street, Glasgow, C.2.
Published by WALTER S. MILLER, 140 Broomfield Road, Glasgow, N.1.

1958, September

for a major position in the financial page of a quality paper, but I was rather shattered to find the other members of staff in the financial section dressed most informally and some even seemed to be clad in clothing more suitable for doing the garden. This very smart bowler hat was placed into the top of a cupboard and for all I know may still be there.

However, Mr Sherret took me to see the editor – the celebrated James Holborn – who explained that far from being a problem, my candidature was an honour which should not be disregarded.

Once again I had to make contact with the local Conservatives. Their rooms, rather less significant than Glasgow Central, were located in an old shop in Atlas Street and it was clear within a few minutes that the organisation consisted largely of a delightful and enthusiastic middle aged lady called Mrs Barclay, whose sons had been at the High School with me, and an elderly chairman whose main function in life seemed to be taking bottles of whisky out of his briefcase and offering refreshment to all those around him.

However, they were overjoyed to hear that I intended to put up a fight and that I could bring along with me a major campaign team - consisting of Eric, who was over 6 feet in height, and the massed ranks of the Townhead Young Conservatives. The Irvine family were again available because they actually resided in Springburn, and at times we had over a dozen helpers available for election duty. The campaign was a real joy with these wonderful helpers. Our enthusiasm knew no bounds and somehow Mrs Barclay always seemed to have cups of tea and cakes for us all when we returned from our leafleting. In addition, being a by-election, we had occasional help from other constituencies and from some councillors.

Like the Townhead campaign, it was quite easy for the candidate. I did not have to shake any hands or kiss any babies. The only direct contact I had with constituents was two visits, arranged by Mrs Barclay, to a local Protestant Minister and a Parish Priest and a rather confusing meeting with an official from the local Orange Lodge. This latter meeting got off to a rather bad start because he started asking about my views on the Union and I foolishly concluded that he was talking about trade unions and advised that I did not have much time for them. He obviously concluded that we were not on the same wavelength, and the prospects of securing some great block vote had to be abandoned.

The only other contact with a constituent I can remember was in a local tearoom restaurant. A waitress came along to our table and asked most respectfully if I was the Tory candidate. Not wishing to confuse the polite girl with a tale about the differences between Progressives and Tories, I simply admitted that this was indeed the case. "I told her that you were", she exclaimed, pointing to the person who was obviously in charge, but she said you could not be because you only ordered pie and beans!"

This somehow conveyed, in a nutshell, all the image problems of Tories and Progressives in Glasgow, in a way that detailed political surveys could not.

The by-election was, on the face of it, a total triumph. The Labour majority was reduced from about 3,000 to about 400 and we sang all the way back from the count to the Rooms where we had the kind of celebration not seen in the Springburn Conservative Rooms for decades. Of course we entirely disregarded the fact that instead of the normal 35 per cent poll in local elections, only 11 per cent of the voters had bothered to turn up and our Constituency Chairman made ample use of his briefcase and the enclosed bottles – his only sadness being that I was not willing to participate. I had, I explained signed the pledge to desist from all alcohol at an early age and Conservatives of all people had to keep their promises.

Immediately, I was asked by the Constituency if I would come back in May to fight again in Cowlairs. Now that the majority in this Labour stronghold was down to 400, another little push of the dynamic Teddy Taylor and his Townhead team would enable the Springburn folk to haul up the Progressive flag in the heart of Labour's badlands.

I doubt if Springburn had ever seen such activity as it did over the next few months. Eric Abell had meantime secured a job and my new agent was Bobby Rowan – a school-friend and joint proprietor of a long established family firm in Glasgow, selling electrical goods, wholesale.

We put in a terrific effort. We even had a special pamphlet to hand to people as they went in to vote, quite apart from the pamphlets thrust through their doors, and, from their limited coffers, the Springburn Tories found the cash to book a huge billboard on the Springburn Road with the slogan "Teddy for Cowlairs".

But disaster lay ahead. The moribund Labour Party, who had never bothered to fight for years, got their act together. There was a near 40 per cent poll instead of the 11 per cent in the by-election, and the Labour majority climbed back to its previous level.

Of course we were all shattered and disillusioned.

There was gloom and despondency in the Rooms, but such was the spirit and fellowship of our team that there was no recrimination. Nobody was made a scapegoat. There was just a feeling of dull resignation and an acceptance that Davids just do not kill Goliaths in the 20th Century, particularly in Glasgow. So what would I do now? Of course I assured the Springburn folk that I would always be available to fight Cowlairs till kingdom come, and I think that they would willingly have run up and down the stairs for me for decades if I had asked them to do so.

Again, my career seemed to have come to a halt, but again by a wonderful accident, a new opportunity created itself. This was Harold Macmillan's decision to call a General Election in 1959.

TUESDAY, 5th MAY

COWLAIRS WARD

THE PROGRESSIVE
Candidate

Edward M.
TAYLOR, M.A.

TO THE ELECTORS OF COWLAIRS WARD

Dear Elector,

I write to you once again as the Progressive Party candidate for this Ward and invite your vote and active support at the forthcoming Election. I was greatly encouraged by the result of the By-Election last December and wish to thank all those who supported me at that time.

You must all be aware of the irresponsibility and folly with which the Labour Town Council has managed our City's affairs—its record, after almost a decade of rule, is one of ever-increasing expenditure and rapidly declining efficiency. When we consider that Glasgow's rates have now reached the all-time "high" of £1 8s. 1d. (compared with 15s 4d. in 1950 when my Party was in power), that transport fares are again being increased and that the Transport and Housing deficits continue to rise, it becomes clear that we are not receiving value for our money.

This Election will be a momentous one for Glasgow, for the choice which you will make on the 5th of May will determine the future of our City. At present we are faced with the prospect of losing 250,000 citizens in the Overspill Plan. The Progressive Party believes that more study is required in this matter before we can agree to "exile" a quarter of our population.

We have faith in the future greatness of Glasgow and seek a mandate from you—its citizens—to govern it wisely and efficiently in the interests of all.

If you show your confidence in me and my Party by electing me on **5th May**, I promise that I will do all in my power to attend to your interests and problems as well as those of Glasgow.

Yours sincerely,

EDWARD M. TAYLOR.

1959, May

BOOK T[

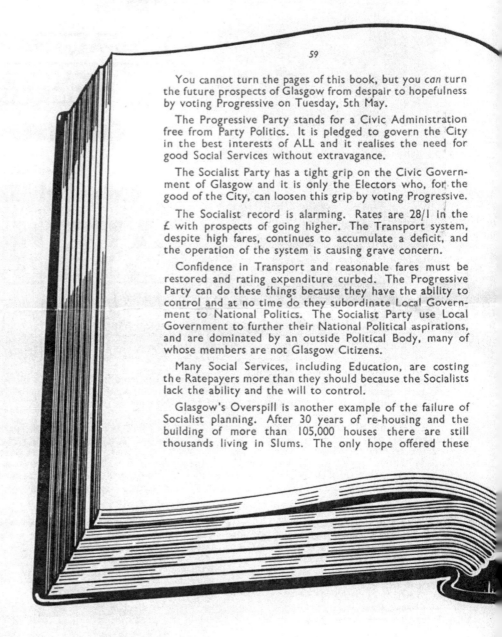

59

You cannot turn the pages of this book, but you *can* turn the future prospects of Glasgow from despair to hopefulness by voting Progressive on Tuesday, 5th May.

The Progressive Party stands for a Civic Administration free from Party Politics. It is pledged to govern the City in the best interests of ALL and it realises the need for good Social Services without extravagance.

The Socialist Party has a tight grip on the Civic Government of Glasgow and it is only the Electors who, for the good of the City, can loosen this grip by voting Progressive.

The Socialist record is alarming. Rates are 28/1 in the £ with prospects of going higher. The Transport system, despite high fares, continues to accumulate a deficit, and the operation of the system is causing grave concern.

Confidence in Transport and reasonable fares must be restored and rating expenditure curbed. The Progressive Party can do these things because they have the ability to control and at no time do they subordinate Local Government to National Politics. The Socialist Party use Local Government to further their National Political aspirations, and are dominated by an outside Political Body, many of whose members are not Glasgow Citizens.

Many Social Services, including Education, are costing the Ratepayers more than they should because the Socialists lack the ability and the will to control.

Glasgow's Overspill is another example of the failure of Socialist planning. After 30 years of re-housing and the building of more than 105,000 houses there are still thousands living in Slums. The only hope offered these

Vote Progressive o[

1959, May

42

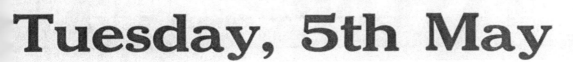

60

people is to leave Glasgow for places as far afield as Wick and Stranraer. Industry also is to be put out of Glasgow because of Socialist failure to so order our land use whereby sites could have been available to keep Glasgow Industry in Glasgow.

The Progressive approach would be to concentrate on developing gap sites and re-siting industry within the City. This, with clearing the worst Slums, should be our first concern. Only after every practical alternative has been adopted should Overspill be accepted as inevitable. Glasgow is a closely integrated workshop. Its re-development should aim at maintaining and improving its contribution to British Industry.

For years the Progressive Party has called for a review of Corporation House Rents. The Socialists, because of National Political motives, refused, and the unfair system of heavy subsidies from the Rates has continued. Due to Progressive insistence the Government ordered an Enquiry and rents have now been reviewed. Prior to the Enquiry the average rent of a Corporation House was 5/2 per week. The average is now 8/- per week. The Electors must judge whether or not this increase is just and reasonable or whether it is merely a reluctant gesture.

The Progressive Party believe that the Corporation Housing List should be re-examined and only those who have resided in Glasgow for many years retained. The inflow of applicants other than really deserving cases should be restricted so that many who have waited so patiently would have a first chance of obtaining a house.

You cannot close this book but you *can* begin a brighter and a better Chapter for Glasgow by voting Progressive on Tuesday, 5th May.

Tuesday, 5th May

1959, May

Vote for Progress — Vote Progressive
Vote TAYLOR for Cowlairs

Election Meeting

MONDAY, 4th MAY

Unionist Rooms
17 Atlas Street
Springburn

At 8 p.m.

All electors are welcome at
this meeting and your candidate
and other prominent speakers
will be present to answer questions

COWLAIRS BY-ELECTION

December 1958

LABOUR MAJORITY—371

This time we fight to win—

Use your Vote wisely

COMMITTEE ROOMS:

17 Atlas Street

1950—15s. 4d.

1954—£1 0s. 4d.

1957—£1 4s. 2d.

1959—£1 8s. 1d.

Recognise these figures ?
These are Glasgow's Rates
We believe your RATES could be CUT

Give us your Support

Labour's Transport Record

Higher Fares
Bigger Losses
Fewer Passengers
Poorer Services

Don't you think it's

Time for a Change ?

Vote thus

TAYLOR, Edward M.	X

Published by HENRY DOBSON, Election Agent, 177 Auchentoshan Terrace, Springburn, N.1.
Printed by C. L. WRIGHT LTD., 100 West George Street, Glasgow, C.2.

5

In the shipyards

When the General Election was announced, the thought of standing as a candidate just never entered my mind. I had, in the meantime changed jobs from the Glasgow Herald to being on the staff of the Clyde Shipbuilders Association. How this happened was that there was a daily routine in the commercial Editorial Staff at the beginning of each day to look at the "situations vacant" page in the paper. Journalists were not terribly well paid in those days and many of the staff in the commercial page were middle aged and had landed up in what seemed to be a backwater. The media opportunities of TV had just not emerged and the dream of every staff member was to secure a position as a Public Relations Director of a State Board like electricity or gas. Private enterprise was just too uncertain and probably too competitive. Nothing seemed quite so exciting as getting a highly paid cushy number in a Public Board and issuing occasional press statements that new power stations were being opened and that Government Ministers were paying visits to gas works.

I felt obliged to join in the daily ritual and was delighted to see that the Clyde Shipbuilders Association was advertising for a clerical assistant at a salary £100 more per annum than I was receiving in the Herald. Apart from the extra cash, the hours were normal and would make it easier for me to attend political meetings in Townhead and Springburn.

The job was secured after a brief interview and I think that there could not have been a better vehicle for making contact with people at all levels of industry. The CSA was not only a trade association, but also the vehicle though which wages and working conditions were resolved in all the Clyde Shipyards.

Basically, when workers and management had a problem, the agreed procedure called for the matter to be considered between the local management and shop stewards. If this did not succeed in resolving the problem, there had to be a Yard Conference. At this conference there would be a full time official of the Trade Union concerned and an official of the CSA. If they did not agree, a local conference was held round a table in our office at which local union leaders and local employers would endeavour to settle things. In extreme cases of disagreement, there could be a National Conference in London where the Federation officials and National union leaders would thrash things out.

Some issues obviously started at local level – for example, if the boilermakers of the Clyde considered that they had a case for a local pay rise overall - and some started nationally like the National pay awards.

It was a time when shipbuilding was just emerging from a period of intense prosperity and beginning to face up to the problems which have virtually decimated the industry since. There were about twenty Yards in the Clyde – most being privately owned, although some like the Yarrows and John Browns were public companies. Many of the bosses were from the old families, like the Connells and the Stephens.

It was a proud industry, but clearly one which had not changed with the times and while we were haggling over how many extra pence should be paid to shipwrights for launches, the tricky Japanese were just beginning to build up their super new shipyards where high technology and superb efficiency would eventually destroy us. In addition, there was a trend towards the giant tankers and other vessels which the Clyde just could not build because of the size of vessel which could be launched in the river.

The job brought me into direct contact with the Union officials of the Clyde and with major employers. At first I went along with senior officials of the CSA to sit in at meetings, my task being to take copious notes to be used as a basis for producing the eventual report which would be circulated round all members. There was a kind of standard formula. We had to first establish who was at the meeting. Then we had to set out the argument for the claim, the employers' reply and then the details of the negotiation. The conclusion was always either the settlement or a decision to "fail to agree" which meant that the next stage of procedure would be undertaken. In the fullness of time, however, I was sent to meetings myself.

Sometimes it seemed to be a bit of a farce, but perhaps a necessary one. I would phone up the union official to see how we might resolve a dispute. We might agree after a while that 3d per hour extra would resolve it, but when the meeting took place, the union official would put forward a mighty and impassioned argument for an extra 6d per hour. I would have to reply with a devastating explanation of the financial problems facing the industry and suggest that no increase was possible. Then we would have an exchange of views and a private adjournment. Eventually we would agree to 3d per hour, and so we all justified ourselves. The union rep would explain to his men that while the hard faced employers had been unwilling to pay a penny, he had managed to secure the 3d increase and I would explain to the employers that while the irresponsible unions had demanded 6d per hour, I had managed to reduce it to 3d.

My experience of the shipyards made me realise what a rotten job it was to be a union official. The members expected their representatives to be in the office all day to answer their problems. They expected them to turn out regularly for evening branch and other meetings and they paid wages to union officials which were often well below the wages being negotiated for the membership.

Some of the union officials I dealt with have gone on to high office – men like John Chalmers of the Boilermakers. They were all hard working and committed men, but they had an immense task in securing the agreement of their membership to anything that might appear to be change and progress. It was this inherent conservatism, and unwillingness to change, which spelt the death of Clydeside; it certainly was not the responsibility of the union officials.

I can well remember, for example, a conference about the introduction of a new Sicomat burning machine. It was a splendid device. Instead of a marker doing a chalk drawing of a hole to be cut on a plate, the Sicomat simply called for a chap in the drawing office to do a small-scale drawing. This was put in the machine, along with the plate; the machine magically and automatically cut out the hole in seconds. All that was required was for an unskilled person to put the drawing in and then to press the "on" button, but the local union branch insisted that the machine had to be manned by two people because it was replacing two tradesmen – highly qualified after five years of apprenticeship.

We pleaded with the unions that this was a bit daft because there was only one seat on the machine and an "on" button did not call for the kind of skills acquired by tradesmen. The union officials seemed anxious to help but were mandated by branch meetings to black the new machines until dual manning was agreed.

Eventually we comprised by agreeing that the new machine would have to be manned by a tradesman and an apprentice tradesman. I often wondered what the poor apprentice did with himself and where he eventually sat. This, in a nutshell, was the problem of the shipyards. Having gone through a time of cost plus contracts and prosperity, the system just did not provide for the kind of changes demanded by new circumstances.

One small contribution, which I helped to secure, was on supervisory training. The procedure in the yards was that when a foreman supervisor died or retired, one of the men in the team was simply appointed to replace him. It was difficult for someone who had been a member of the team or squad one day to acquire the authority to manage the next.

I was sent by the CSA to the Chesters College to seek out a suitable course for aspiring foremen. A most unusual course was devised which included all kinds of subjects like the make up of public companies, social anthropology and banking practice. My report suggested that the course would be of little value to any shipyard employee directly but that it could do a power of good to the morale and authority of a potential supervisor to have been to college. My recommendation was accepted and I often wonder how the lads enjoyed their studies.

When I visit Glasgow from time to time and see the devastation in what used to be a thriving industry, I often wonder if any steps could have been taken to prevent the virtual collapse of a once great industry.

What was the factor which stopped the new techniques being introduced? Why were the men so unwilling to agree to changes which could have made the future prospects brighter? Why was there so little trust between management and workpeople?

Obviously it is a complex issue which could in itself justify a book, but I think there is just a clue from the success of some American companies in areas where traditional industries have such little success.

Communications are a near obsession with the US firms with everyone knowing what is happening and why. They seem to care for individuals more, with effort being recognised and rewarded. There are lots of detailed examples which I could give but perhaps the most telling was the US Levi Company which made jeans. They had a delightful practice of having an award evening for their young trainees in a posh hotel to which parents were invited and the young girls, many of whom had probably never attained any real success in school or elsewhere, were given merit certificates for their achievements by a senior representative of the company and then handed bouquets of flowers as they walked off the platform. This small but terribly kindly recognition of achievement seemed to secure a kind of employee loyalty which was in a different world from the shipyards, where a watch for 30 years service seemed to be the extent of recognition.

6

Standing for Parliament

But back to the world of politics.

The General Election had been called and my immediate thought was how we could harness the enthusiasms of the Townhead Young Conservatives to support whoever would be chosen as the Parliamentary candidate. I also joined the local Party in Cathcart - where I lived - which was still a Conservative seat although the building of the huge Castlemilk housing estate scheme within its borders was causing some anxiety.

In the meantime there was excitement in Springburn. The normal procedure for selecting candidates in the more difficult seats was that the Party would send a brief note of some candidates who were available and sometimes would make a specific recommendation. The list was sent to the Springburn Tories and they had a meeting of the committee to look at them.

The old Chairman, Mr Adams, may have had a bad day but the outcome was, that they decided to send a note to the Party saying that none of the candidates offered by the Party were acceptable. Normally local constituency parties would not dare question the authority of the local party HQ but the Springburn folk had perhaps got a bit full of themselves after all the excitement and media coverage of the Cowlairs by-election. Also there was a natural reaction against the kind of candidates who were normally available to fight the "hopeless seats". They often tended to be the well- connected chaps, with double-barrelled names, from the counties outside Glasgow who felt that a contest in a difficult seat was a necessary but disagreeable apprenticeship to being considered for one of the safer seats in the counties.

In any event, the Springburn folk decided to be "bolshie" and the delightful Mrs Barclay suggested that instead they would like me to be their candidate. They did not advise me of their decision, but I had a friendly phone call from Central Office asking what it was all about. They explained in the most courteous of tones that I could not be considered because I was not on the candidates' list.

This was the first I had heard about the Springburn decision, but the next day I had a phone call from Mrs Barclay saying that the Springburn folk were adamant that I had to stand. Apparently, there was a crisis meeting with the Springburn executive in which the position was explained to them. While TT might indeed be a good chap, it was not possible for them to have an official candidate who was not on the list.

But the Springburn folk insisted.

There was then a whole series of complex phone calls and discussions but eventually it emerged that I was to be considerd for the candidates list and happily I was approved. I was then officially selected by the Springburn Association.

The campaign was really exciting. The highlight of the Glasgow campaign was a great rally in the Odeon cinema addressed by the Prime Minister and as the youngest candidate – I was then 22 – I was invited to second the vote of thanks Motion.

It was quite an experience to be at a meeting where there was such fantastic enthusiasm. If Harold Macmillan had read out the notes from the gardening column of the parish magazine, the huge audience would have cheered him to the echo. All the Glasgow candidates were seated in the front row of the platform and we were introduced one by one. All of us were cheered as though we were about to embark on the great crusade to relieve Jerusalem and there were Union Jacks and booming organ music playing patriotic airs. Andrew Strang was a wizard in many ways, but organising the great political rallies was his special forte. It was all very exciting, but I soon found that a Parliamentary Election was rather different from a local battle.

For a start there were public meetings at which voters did actually turn up and I had to deal with complex questions relying on the notes posted daily from the Party headquarters, and one also had to deal with the unusual questions from the cranks who seemed to take joy in election meetings.

I well remember one which really stumped me – a wizened old chap with a walking stick who stood up waving a bundle of papers who put the question to me:-

"Is the candidate in favour of abolishing money – yes or no?" I had been schooled on the importance of not antagonising voters and so I gave a most general and reassuring reply that it was an interesting idea which I could perhaps discuss with him after the meeting. Of course it did not really help because he simply turned up the next night with the same question and was clearly far from being satisfied with the revised Taylor answer of "It all depends what you mean by money".

Then there were the hosts of letters and questionnaires. They all had to be answered, we had been told at the candidates' meetings, and so the bodies seeking to establish Plumbers Registration Councils, to abolish fox-hunting, and to give higher pensions to naval ex-servicemen all had to get replies. Then there was the Press.

Reporters turned up to assess the campaign, anxious to get some new angle in what was inevitably a rather boring national campaign. What were the issues in Springburn? How did we feel about the electoral response?

Then there was a joint meeting with the Labour candidate organised by a local church. The sitting MP was a wily old gentleman called John Foreman who had never made much of an impact in Westminster but who clearly was well known in the area. There was an astonishing amount of abuse for a meeting in a church.

I can recall one voter, who was patiently requested by the clergyman in the chair to "Please put a question", just saying with obvious sincerity that "Tories are rubbish". There was even a proposal from another which met with unexpected enthusiasm to the effect that "There was a place for Taylor in Springburn, but it has not been dug yet!" But there were nice people too.

Dear Mrs Barclay was constantly cheering me up with tales of people she had met who had always voted Labour but had decided to change over and support me, and I had the additional bonus of having as my election agent a really committed person called Gordon Rennie who later was to secure victory as a councillor in the traditional Labour Ward of Woodside and literally to work himself to an early death with his total devotion to his constituents. Gordon held three surgeries per week to see people with problems; at some there were more than 50 callers.

The campaign went well and we managed to get over 10,000 votes which was regarded as a good result even although the Labour candidate got several thousand more.

10, Downing Street,
Whitehall.

October 8, 1959.

Dear Mr Taylor

This is just to thank you very much for
proposing the vote of thanks at my meeting in
Glasgow.   If I may say so, I thought that your
speech was just right for the occasion.

I wish you the best of luck in your contest.
You deserve to win, and I have every hope that
you will do so.

Yours sincerely
Harold Macmillan

E.M. Taylor, Esq.
From the Prime Minister, October, 1959

Of course there was disappointment. Even in the most hopeless of seats, the candidates always have a sneaking feeling that things might just work out in a miraculous way, but on a personal basis, I had "made a mark", and the Press and radio reported that the campaign for Springburn had gone well. TT, some stated, was a person to watch.

7

Becoming a Councillor

I might well have soldiered on in the Springburns of this world forever, but for another piece of good fortune. I lived in the Cathcart Ward of the Cathcart Constituency and it had always been a Progressive stronghold. In fairness, things were rather more difficult because of the building of the giant housing scheme which was actually bigger than the city of Perth. In consequence, the Cathcart Ward had no less than 25,000 voters – and was said to be the largest in Scotland.

Being a safe seat, the Party did not allocate candidates. The selection was made by the Ward Committee – a kind of community council which was entirely non-political but who despite this, had the task of selecting the Progressive candidate.

I was never sure how the Ward Committee actually secured this task and entitlement. What seems to have happened, is that the Committee, for which there was one in each ward in Glasgow, had adopted the practice of recommending a candidate, and because the Progressive Party did not have any local organisation at all and therefore no local election committee, the Ward Committee somehow took on the job. There were members of the committee who were active Labour members, and it seemed strange that they took part in the selection. However, that is how it happened.

A dear and popular old councillor called Andrew Donald died in December of 1959 and a by-election had to be called in January 1960. Two potential candidates were in the field including one who was a member of the Committee. Some others

Give the young fellow a chance!

Come and Hear the young man's point of view from

TEDDY TAYLOR

The **UNIONIST** Candidate

FOR

SPRINGBURN

Wed. 30th Sept.
ST. MARTHA'S SCHOOL — Menzies Road
PROVANMILL (TEMPORARY) — Robroyston Road

Thurs. 1st Oct.
COLSTON SECONDARY — Springburn Road
PETERSHILL SECONDARY — Petershill Road

Fri. 3rd Oct.
SPRINGBURN SCHOOL — Gourlay Street
BALGRAY SCHOOL — Red Road

Mon. 5th Oct.
GADBURN PRIMARY — 70 Rockfield Road
BALORNOCK PRIMARY ANNEXE — Edgefauld Rd.

Tues. 6th Oct.
ELMVALE — Hawthorn Street
ALBERT SECONDARY — Mansel Street

Eve of Poll Rally

SPRINGBURN HALL

WEDNESDAY, 7th OCTOBER at 8 p.m.

Published by J. GORDON RENNIE, Election Agent, 17 Atlas Street, Glasgow, N.I.
Printed by K. & R. DAVIDSON, LIMITED 205-207 West George Street, Glasgow, C.2.

1959, October

58

Parliamentary Election, 1959   **Springburn Division**

A PERSONAL MESSAGE

from

EDWARD TAYLOR

Unionist Candidate

POLLING DAY : THURSDAY 8TH OCTOBER

1959, October

17 Atlas Street,
Springburn.

October, 1959.

Dear Elector,

My friends in Springburn have asked me to offer myself as a Candidate to represent you in Parliament. I am proud to accept this invitation and I ask for YOUR support.

It is now nearly eight years since the Unionist Party became responsible for the Government of Britain; and I am sure that you will agree that, in this time, much progress has been made in cutting Taxation, building more Houses, Schools and Hospitals, halting the rise in the Cost of Living and working for Peace. Will YOU give us a chance to continue with this Progress?

I am well aware that Springburn has its own special problems at this time. If you elect me as your Member I promise that these problems would be voiced vigorously and frequently in Parliament and that I shall do all in my power to attend to your interests as well as those of Britain.

Yours sincerely,

Edward Taylor

About Your Candidate . . .

At 22 years of age EDWARD TAYLOR is the youngest Candidate standing in the present General Election. This is not a disadvantage as he is able to look on problems with the eyes and mind of a young man which is a tremendous help in this age of progress and change.

He graduated with Honours from Glasgow University over a year ago and at present is training for a career in Industrial Relations.

Edward Taylor's background as a Candidate is not however purely academic. He contested Townhead Ward for the Progressive Party in May 1958 and many people there remember the young Candidate who fought so well under the slogan of "Teddy Taylor for Townhead". In December 1958 and again in May 1959 he contested Cowlairs Ward and was responsible for a substantial reduction in the Labour majority. He is keenly interested in, and alive to all the many problems in the constituency, problems of housing, redundancy and employment in particular. He knows the problems of the old people and of the younger people and is determined that Springburn will not be left out of any Government schemes to bring new work to the area. He is a Sunday School teacher in his Church.

This is what We have done

BALANCE OF PAYMENTS.—Under the Unionist Government we have earned abroad £1,600 m. **MORE** than we have spent. Exports have reached the highest peak ever. The economy is sounder than at any time since the war.

COST OF LIVING.—Prices are steady and many are coming down.

PROSPERITY.—People are earning more, saving more, eating more, and buying more.

TAXATION.—Income Tax and Purchase Tax have been reduced. Tax on Sport and Theatre has been abolished.

EMPLOYMENT.—Despite a World recession employment has remained at a high level.

HOUSES.—Labour said that we could NOT build 300,000 Houses in one year. We DID! School building has also been stepped up.

PENSIONS.—Three rises in the Old Age Pension—from 30/- to 50/-. The Pension is now worth 10/6d. more in buying power than in 1951.

In the international field, thanks to Mr. Macmillan's initiative, the deadlock between East and West has been broken.

This is what We shall do

EMPLOYMENT.—In Scotland the emphasis will be on **JOBS.** Scotland's over-dependence on the old-established heavy industries, has resulted, even in prosperous times in a relatively higher rate of unemployment. **We pledge ourselves to work to correct this by attracting new industries to areas where they are needed.**

HOUSING.—By 1965 we intend to rehouse, at least, another million people from the slums. We will press on with providing new houses and jobs for Glasgow families moving out of the crowded parts of the city. Another new town will be built if this proves necessary.

WELFARE.—Reforms in mental health, a major expansion in hospital buildings and a massive school building programme are planned for Scotland.

SCIENCE.—The development of Nuclear Energy for **peaceful purposes** will be pushed ahead.

TRANSPORT.—Under the Railway programme 3,000 new Diesels will be in service by 1965, 8,000 miles of track relaid and electric traction increased by 60%.

NATIONALISATION.—We are opposed to any extension of Nationalisation; we shall strive to improve the commercial standards of Nationalised Industries.

PENSIONS.—We pledge ourselves to ensure that Pensioners continue to share in the good things which a steadily expanding economy will bring.

PEACE.—We will continue to work unceasingly for a lasting Peace and for World Disarmament.

Life is better under the Unionists Don't let Labour Ruin it!

1959, October

SPRINGBURN DIVISION

Give the YOUNG Fellow a chance

VOTE TAYLOR

Vote Unionist

18th September, 1959.

Dear Taylor,

I am sending you this personal message to wish you all success on October 8th.

Our policy since 1951 has expanded this country's prosperity and placed it on firmer foundations than for decades past. The British people today are earning and saving more than ever before; they are benefiting from the tax cuts of seven Budgets; and for the first time for many a long year they are enjoying the double blessing of full employment and steady prices.

Eight years ago Sir Winston Churchill described our policy as "setting the people free". Our policy in the next five years is to keep the people free, and to use the fruits of freedom for a great constructive programme which will raise still further our own standards of life and leisure and keep faith with the Commonwealth countries who look to us for a helping hand.

A Socialist Government now would place all our hard won gains at risk. Free enterprise does practically all of our export trade; it provides directly or indirectly the greater part of the money we spend on the social services; most people depend on it for their jobs. Yet this is the system which our opponents are itching to nationalise, in one way or another, and submit to bureaucratic control.

Prosperity at home depends on Peace abroad.

I hope your electors will continue to entrust us with the tasks to which we have set our hands.

Yours sincerely,

Harold Macmillan

1959, October

on the Committee and one of the two remaining Ward Councillors were unhappy about the way the decision was likely to go and so I had a phone call asking if I would be willing to present myself, as a possible candidate, to the Ward Committee. This was an exciting prospect because selection would be a virtual guarantee of election. However, the local councillor told me that I would not have a chance of being selected (although you could never tell) but that it would be good experience for me in appearing before other such committees.

So I sent of an official application to the Ward Committee, having received an assurance from the Councillors that as all the meetings of the Council took place during the lunch hour, there should be no great problem with my job. There were three candidates up for the selection. The favourite was a Mr David McKellar, a most genuine and active member of the community and a local post office official. However, what distressed the other local councillors was that he had never stood for the Progressive Party as a candidate anywhere. They thought that this was not quite right. How could he be relied upon to back the Party in the City Chambers?

The second applicant was an experienced candidate who had somehow managed never to win elsewhere.

We all gave a little speech, and I stressed the simple fact that I had lived in the area all my life and had experience of fighting both local and Parliamentary contests. The questions were friendly and courteous. What were my special interests in council activities? Would my job enable me to have the time to attend Council meetings? Would I make a practice of attending the Ward Committee meetings each month to report back on what was happening in the Council?

The candidates then retired and I am told, although I do not exactly know, that there was a sharp disagreement between those who wanted the local man – David McKellar – and those who wanted the experienced Party candidate who lived in another part of Glasgow.

It was because the disagreements could not be resolved, that the kindly chairman, Mr Hunter, suggested that the obvious compromise would be to select me as someone who was both local and an experienced candidate.

The three of us, who were sitting in a side room awaiting the decision with anxiety, were all rather astonished to be told that I was the lucky candidate.

Having assured my parents and my employer that there was really little, if any, prospect of my being selected, I was rather taken aback, but got down immediately to plan the campaign.

I have always been really lucky in having good and kindly friends throughout my political career and Mr Hunter suggested that as David McKellar was obviously distressed by the decision it might be a nice gesture to offer him the post of election agent. He would be unlikely to accept, but it was nevertheless sensible to ask.

Again, to my surprise, David agreed, and this was the basis of a long lasting friendship.

However I was soon to find out that standing as a candidate in a safe seat was a wholly different ball game from standing for a hopeless one. In all the previous contests, my helpers and advisers had been kindly, understanding and perhaps subservient. If I, as candidate, wanted something to be done, whether it was the wording of a pamphlet or the issuing of a press statement, nobody ever seemed to question it, but in the "safe" seat, you are immediately confronted by a whole series of people who seem to regard the seat and the campaign as their property. Far from being the "king", I was the temporary tenant of a property which belonged to those who had built it up with the sweat of their brows and their task was to ensure that I did not damage the property by any action or activity.

These kindly Progressive leaders who had offered nothing but friendship and help in Townhead and Springburn seemed to be transformed into interfering and critical supervisors who demanded the right to ensure that nothing which I said or did would undermine the sanctity or security of their safe seat. While Springburn and Townhead had seemed to belong to me, Cathcart belonged, it seemed to the Progressive Party and to the Conservatives locally, who were obviously anxious to ensure that the majorities in local government wards were maintained.

There were many battles. The biggest one was over what we should do about Castlemilk.

The Ward had basically two parts. The older part – largely owner occupied but just beginning to deteriorate a bit socially as the managers and professional people moved to the suburbs outside the City boundaries. The other part, slightly larger and growing, was the giant Castlemilk housing estate, which consisted entirely of rows and rows of four story tenements and about seven blocks of multi-storey flats. It was for all practical purposes a "new town" which had been built to re-house those made homeless by the bulldozing of the central areas of the city.

The general strategy in Cathcart elections had

been to activate the older parts of the Ward and to leave the large scheme entirely alone, in the hope that the lack of political activity would create the maximum apathy.

I immediately rebelled against this. My campaign in Castlemik was going to be as active as my campaign in old Cathcart and it was vital to capture the hearts and minds of the new residents.

This led to some furious rows as I was advised that while I had every right to cut my own throat, it was the height of irresponsibility to destroy the electoral chances of the other two councillors who would face election in the next two years and was wholly unfair to the MP, whose seat could be in danger if the Socialist hordes of Castlemilk were to discover the route to the polling stations.

Within a few days, it became clear that those who had selected the "nice young man" as a compromise candidate and who had given me a chance denied to others of standing in other Wards were realising fast that instead they had selected a rather impossible and arrogant immature person who was not willing to listen to reason or good advice.

But I did not lack allies.

Slowly but surely a group of fellow "establishment bashers" began to gather round and within a short while we had the creation of what came to be known as the Cathcart mafia. If there was a common theme to the mafia, it was that we had to stir up the rather sleepy Conservative and Progressive Parties, and that the role of the Party had to be to create and build up support in the traditional Labour strongholds.

The by-election proceeded and the result was satisfactory. Of course our little mafia group insisted that we had succeeded in securing votes in Castlemilk and that what had been achieved there could be done throughout the City.

What a fantastic election team we established.

Jimmy Anderson was in some ways the king pin. He was a master of election organisation and was later to become a councillor for Cathcart and a Chairman of the Police Committee in a glorious year when the Progressives had a great victory in Glasgow. There was John Young, again to be a Cathcart Councillor and Leader of the Conservative Group and who was eventually to become a member of the Scottish Parliament. There was the other John Young, an expert in propaganda and the production of campaign leaflets and slogans – an expertise secured from his job as Deputy Editor of a local evening newspaper. Names like those of Willie Shearer, Walter Whitehill, Jeannie Macan, Jim Ewing and Jack Richmond all convey an image of excitement and vitality to those who engaged in Glasgow politics, and in Castlemilk itself we built up a huge and successful Conservative Branch led by Len Gourlay, a tough and wiry enthusiast who again became a councillor himself. There was Eric Olivarios, manager of a local engineering company, and his wife Mary and a remarkable retired policeman called Dougie McGillivray who was to become Organising Secretary of the Conservatives. Also in Tom and Maude Potter we had an example of a most delightful and kindly couple living in the best part of the Ward who, although older, had the unique capacity of a small part of that age group to rejoice in the activity of the young Turks. We established a movement of "hit squad" as it was called by our political enemies, which enjoyed running campaigns in Labour Heartland seats.

There were over the next few months some staggering results.

Fairfield was the safest of Labour seats in the heart of the shipyards consisting of grim tenement

Tuesday, 19th January
(CATHCART WARD)

THE PROGRESSIVE CANDIDATE
EDWARD M. TAYLOR
M.A.

TO THE ELECTORS OF CATHCART WARD

DEAR ELECTOR,

This by-election has been caused by the death of Councillor Andrew Donald who represented Cathcart faithfully and with distinction for fifteen years. His wise counsel and sincere dedication will be sadly missed in the Council Chamber and especially in the Education and Health and Welfare Committees where he rendered outstanding service throughout his term of office.

Democracy, however, requires that you choose another person to represent you in the City's Council and I am proud to have been invited by the Cathcart Ward Committee and the Glasgow Progressive Party to stand as a candidate with their support in the forthcoming Election.

You must be aware of the irresponsibility and folly with which the Labour Town Council has managed our City's affairs since it regained power—its record, after almost a decade of unbroken rule, is one of ever-increasing expenditure and rapidly declining efficiency. **When we consider that Glasgow's Rates have reached the alarming level of £1 7s. 8d. (compared with 15s. 4d. in 1950 when my Party was in power), that Transport fares have been recently increased once again and that the Housing and Transport deficits continue to rise, it becomes clear that we are not receiving value for our money.**

The unjust system whereby tenants of privately rented houses and owner-occupiers pay not only for their own houses but also a large part of the rents of Council House tenants, is all too representative of Socialist policies. **A Progressive administration would put an end to this injustice but would introduce an equitable rebate scheme for Council House tenants who could not afford to pay more.**

If you show your confidence in me and my Party by electing me on **Tuesday, 19th January,** I promise that I will do all in my power to attend to your interests and problems as well as those of Glasgow.

Yours sincerely,

EDWARD M. TAYLOR.

1960, January

About your Candidate

Ward Chairman's Message

UNANIMOUS CHOICE

One of the difficulties facing would-be candidates in cities such as Glasgow is the fact that Council and Committee meetings are held in business hours. This restricts the choice of candidates somewhat, and also tends to make the average age on Councils high. It was with particular pleasure that the Cathcart Ward Committee heard that one of the younger residents in its area, who was able to devote adequate time to Council duties, was willing to be considered as a candidate for the by-election caused by the death of Councillor Donald. Mr. Taylor became the unanimous choice of the Committee.

YOUTH ON HIS SIDE

Cathcart Ward Committee is regarded as being one of the most energetic in the City, and includes as one of its prime duties the submission to the electors of the most suitable candidate for each annual election. In Cathcart we have been well served in past years, and Mr. E. Taylor was considered as having all the attributes to make an excellent choice. He has youth on his side, but is already experienced in municipal affairs. I have the additional pleasure of having known him personally for many years, and can unhesitatingly endorse my Committee's recommendation.

ROBERT HUNTER,
Chairman,
Cathcart Ward Committee.

EDWARD TAYLOR is one of the youngest candidates to stand in a Municipal Election. This is no disadvantage as he is able to look on problems with the eyes and mind of a young man which is a tremendous help in this age of progress and change.

He was educated in a Glasgow school and at Glasgow University, where he studied Economics and Politics and graduated with Honours. He is at present training for a career in Industrial Relations.

Edward Taylor's background as a candidate is not, however, purely academic. He contested Townhead Ward for the Progressive Party in May, 1958, and many people there remember the young candidate who fought so well in that Municipal Election. In December, 1958, and again in May, 1959, he contested Cowlairs Ward and was responsible for a substantial reduction in the Labour majority. In the recent General Election, he was the Unionist candidate in the Springburn division.

Having lived in the Cathcart district all his life, he is keenly interested in, and alive to, the many problems in the Ward.

PARTY LEADER'S STATEMENT

Councillor W. Gordon Reid, *Chairman of the Progressive Group in Glasgow Town Council, writes :—*

"As Chairman of the Glasgow Progressive Party, it gives me great pleasure to recommend your support for Mr. Edward Taylor on Election day.

He is the unanimous choice of my Party, and a young man of undoubted ability who is very experienced in municipal and national affairs.

I feel certain that when elected, Mr. Taylor will well and truly attend the affairs of the City in general and Cathcart Ward in particular."

Vote for PROGRESS — Vote PROGESSIVE
Vote EDWARD TAYLOR for Cathcart

VOTE FOR A LOCAL MAN

OVERSPILL

At present we are faced with the prospect of losing over 250,000 citizens under the Overspill Plan. Although some overspill is necessary, the Progressive Party believes that more study is required in this matter before we can agree to "exile" a quarter of our population and thus add to the Rates burden of those who remain.

APATHY POLLS

Municipal by-elections have been notorious for the apathetic response of Electors.

Let your candidate feel that he has a mandate from all Electors in the Ward by ensuring that every member of your family votes Progressive on Election day —

TUESDAY, 19th JANUARY

1950 — 15/4

1954 — £1 0s. 4d.

1957—£1 4s. 2d.

TRANSPORT

Glasgow's transport was once admired throughout Europe. What do you think of it now ?

Vote Progressive for a vigorous drive for efficiency and solvency in the Transport Department.

FOR SOUND ADMINISTRATION

VOTE PROGRESSIVE

VOTE FOR *EDWARD TAYLOR*

1959 — £1 7s. 8d.

Recognise these figures ? These are Glasgow's Rates.

The Progressive Party believes that your Rates could be cut by—

(A) An Energetic Drive for Economy.

(B) An injection of private and business enterprise into Municipal Policy.

(C) An ending of the unjust system whereby tenants and owners of private houses subsidise all tenants of Council houses whether they can afford to pay more or not.

1960, January

TAYLOR *for* CATHCART

WHERE TO HEAR

TUESDAY, 12th JANUARY, 1960
    GLENWOOD SCHOOL, ARDENCRAIG ROAD   8 p.m.

THURSDAY, 14th JANUARY, 1960
    MERRYLEE PRIMARY SCHOOL, FRIARTON ROAD   8 p.m.

FRIDAY, 15th JANUARY, 1960
    CROFTFOOT SCHOOL, CROFTHILL ROAD   8 p.m.

MONDAY, 18th JANUARY, 1960
    COUPER INSTITUTE, CLARKSTON ROAD   8 p.m.

All electors are welcome at these meetings and your candidate and supporting speakers will be present to answer questions.

WHERE TO HELP AND OBTAIN HELP

COMMITTEE ROOMS :

Unionist Rooms, 1 Clarkston Road

HOW TO VOTE

Support the PROGRESSIVE CANDIDATE on

TUESDAY, 19th JANUARY, 1960

VOTE THUS :

TAYLOR, EDWARD M.	

buildings, but we managed to get a local clergyman, Derek Neilson, elected there after a furious campaign which grabbed national headlines. Perhaps the most staggering of all was to win a by-election in Mile End – which Progressives had sometimes never bothered to contest – when Bob Gavin, a Cathcart builder, was elected amidst scenes of wild enthusiasm.

So Cathcart began to get a reputation as a place where a new movement was taking place to stir up the rather sleepy Party. At the National Party Conferences, the Cathcart Young Conservatives, led by a student called Andy Leven, displayed banners and generally drew attention to the Constituency in a way which rather astonished some of the more traditional faces at Perth.

It all seemed to happen very quickly and dramatically, but meantime I had my job to do as a local councillor, and I soon found out that the council work was a different world from the glamour of fighting election contests.

Glasgow Council was at that time an all-purpose Council, with responsibility for the whole range of local services including education, police, fire and water supplies. This was before the massive local government reforms which placed Glasgow in the position of being a district council with limited powers and with the main function going to a giant region covering the West of Scotland.

All the Council meetings took place in the City Chambers between 1pm and 2.30pm and there were committee meetings most days. Within the period it was also possible to get a lunch in the magnificent dining room. Sitting round the large tables, with fellow Progressive Councillors, was a unique education in itself because there we had the people who had the job of running, over the years, the massive responsibilities of a major local government area. The only exception was each alternative Thursday, when there was a meeting of the full council, which tended to go on until about 3.30pm, considering the minutes and reports from the various committees.

As the Press were not permitted to attend committees in these days, but were allowed to attend the General Meeting, the committees tended to be constructive and serious while the General Meeting was boisterous and eventful.

The Labour administration then was quite different from the Labour Councils we see today. The membership tended to be much older and more anxious to take advice from the excellent officials. One had the feeling that the political issues had to be created and sometimes artificially manufactured and there was not a great deal of difference in what Progressive or Labour Councils did except in some key areas, like the scale of council rates. It was only around 1964, when I left the Council to go to Parliament that the proceedings appeared to become more political and ideological. For example, the previous Labour administration had gladly accepted the continuance of five excellent grammar schools in Glasgow and was rather proud of them, but when there was an influx of young ideologists and aspiring Parliamentary candidates, decisions were made to go comprehensive and abolish the old schools.

There was a unique sense of responsibility and civic dignity which seems to have largely gone now. Part of the reason is undoubtedly the change in the character of the Labour Party, but I am in no doubt that another reason was the decision – I believe wholly wrong – of the Conservative Party, to move into local government in Scotland and replace the mixture of Progressives, Moderates and Independents, who generally had upheld basic Conservative ideas in councils.

The introduction of Conservatives did, in my view, make the Labour Party behave more like Socialists and there is also no doubt that the electoral consequences for the Right have been disastrous. Many people who were perfectly willing to vote for local non-socialist parties were simply not willing to support Conservative candidates.

I think that the emergence of harsher party rivalries in local government has not helped the cause of good government because my experience of the Glasgow Council was that there were very few decisions that we had to make which in any sense could be regarded as party political.

I did have just a few problems sitting in all the meetings of the Council with my job in the office, even though the office was just half a mile from the Council building, but my boss was more than understanding and the shipyard bosses seemed to be quite pleased to have "one of their men" in the Council.

While the Council meetings took up a lot of time, the constituency work meant non-stop work in the evenings. As councillors should, I tried to make myself generally available, and the plain fact is that any person or body which makes itself available for consultation and which might be in a position to resolve problems is immediately flooded out with work.

There were tenants associations to meet and there were many letters and phone calls which required visits to constituents' homes. Then there were the pensioners' groups and church groups which were always glad to have a councillor to fill up a syllabus.

The surgeries were hectic. I started the practice of holding a weekly surgery, which soon became two weekly surgeries and it was unusual to have less than 30 attending – the record was 63 one very long Saturday morning. Each caller usually resulted in two letters – one to the person to say what was being done about their problem and the other to the Department from whom advice or help was sought.

The greatest problem I had, apart from time, was a financial one. There were no allowances for councillors and not even provision for postage. I calculated that the direct cost of my council work took up a third of my salary, which is one of the reasons why I am not one of those who criticises daily allowances for councillors. Also I had to learn to type, and before long, the small room in our house, which I used as an office, was full of constituency case files with the copies of letters.

Castlemilk was in itself a full time job. It had a multitude of social and environmental problems, but in some ways, the lifestyle of this working class area with loads of poverty and unemployment was firmer and more secure than the lifestyle in the more affluent 1980s.

Family break up was very rare. The problems which seem so often to lead to family break up were prevented by the extended family. The mothers who just could not cope had the back up of a whole team of grannies, sisters-in-law, sisters and aunts who could step in and take over responsibility for the children, and the horrendous financial pressures of today were just not there. A financial crisis was when a gas bill of £10 could not be paid. Now we have credit cards and bank overdrafts. The fact was that peoples' expectations and those of their children were not so great and I often feel that we have built up huge time bombs to family stability by the manner in which expensive credit facilities are thrust on people. There is no doubt that working class Glaswegians had an infinitely greater sense of obligation to neighbours. Life was not such a rush, fewer women were at work and there was more contact and fellowship between neighbours.

But in Castlemilk, as in the rest of Britain, things had changed. The saddest parts of my visits to Glasgow are to travel round the scheme and see the numbers of empty houses which cannot be let, to learn from the residents that the grim tragedy of family break up is proceeding there as in the rest of the country.

I stood for re-election only once for Cathcart. In the May after my election, councillor Alex Hutton, undoubtedly the outstanding orator of the city chambers, was re-elected, but in the following May, for the first time in history, there was a shock defeat for the sitting councillor, Gordon Reid – leader of the Party – by 26 votes.

So when I stood for re-election in 1962, the Cathcart seat had become a knife-edge battle.

We worked like Trojans to hold the seat. The famous Mafia got down to work in earnest and they faced up to a sizeable Labour organisation which was hungry for another win.

It was a really fierce contest, but we won through with a record majority of over 3,500. I am quite sure that part of the reason was that Conservatives in the old part of Cathcart who had always assumed that the seat was safe, flocked out to the polls after the shock of the previous year's defeat.

But our Mafia insisted that the real reason was, that our policy of initiating real battles in the Labour stronghold was a recipe for victory, and this, justly or unjustly, was what the general interpretation was, and Cathcart had become headline news. Our local activists had the feeling that far from just fighting a local election battle, we were crusading for the soul of the Conservative Party in Scotland.

We had, in short, become a movement.

8

Going to Westminster

As the General Election of 1964 approached, there were anxieties within the Cathcart Conservatives, about the future of the Parliamentary seat. Its boundaries were such that, not only was the Castlemilk housing scheme a major part of the electorate, but also a smaller but quite substantial council scheme with the highly inappropriate name of Toryglen where the Labour Party had become highly organised. In addition, there were feelings that the new aggressive vitality of the Cathcart Conservatives did not fit in with the character of the very kindly but elderly MP John Henderson.

Mr Henderson was ageing and approaches were made to him to stand down, but he was initially not keen to quit the seat. However, after some rather testy meetings with the office bearers and Executive Committee, he agreed to stand down. He was later awarded a knighthood for all his most agreeable public service.

Cathcart had to choose a new candidate and I put myself forward. There were several contenders including George Weir, who was the son of the head of the giant Weir Company which was the major employer in the constituency.

I was eventually chosen as candidate, although it was in no sense an easy victory. Then came the difficult task of fighting the election in a seat which was clearly deteriorating politically like many of the seats within Glasgow's boundaries. This gradual deterioration that has occurred in many cities can be seen from the fact that while in the early 1960s the majority of seats in Glasgow were held by Conservatives, there is not now one Tory representing the city. The last bastion – Hillhead – fell a few years ago to the SDP Roy Jenkins and all the others are now held by Labour.

After a fierce fight, we won Cathcart by a majority of 3,000 although Hillhead was the only other "survivor." It had been a pretty gloomy result overall for the Conservatives with Harold Wilson heading for Downing Street, but for me it was the opening up of a whole new opportunity in going to Westminster.

9

Going to Parliament

I think that most people would assume that new MPs are flooded out with advice about what to do, where to go and how they should conduct themselves. I thought, perhaps foolishly, that after an election result was announced, an official would appear from nowhere with a bulky and important looking envelope with booklets about procedure and passes to meetings, buildings and consultations. In actual fact, nothing happens at all.

I well remember that after the victory party was over, and all the thank you letters sent to election helpers, there was a long pause of several days when I just did not know what to do with myself. I suppose that most MPs have personal friends already in the House, but the only ones I had met had been beaten in the election and I was obviously reluctant to contact them. Quite apart from the mystery of Parliament, I had only been in London once in my life before and that was for a day on the way to a school trip to Switzerland.

Nevertheless we had to make preparations quickly. A Scottish MP has to spend his week in London, travelling up only at weekends to visit his home. The salary was not too good at that time and if expensive accommodation was secured and a full-time secretary employed, there would not be much left. Nowadays, things are much easier for MPs with quite generous allowances being made available on top of salaries for accommodation in London and for the employment of secretaries, but these privileges were not available in 1964.

So it had to be a little guesthouse in Clapham for accommodation which, as it happened, turned out to be an ideal place to live. I discovered it in an advert in *The Sunday Post* and the proprietors, a Mr and Mrs Fair, looked after me in the way in which you would expect a favourite aunt to do. Then however we had the first day in Parliament. Most new MPs feel rather important and significant people when they first arrive in Parliament but, unless the new man is a surprise victor in a by-election, the feeling of importance and significance disappears very fast. You are suddenly thrown into a mass of about 600 people and for the new boy, it is distressing, to say the least, that most of the MPs seem to know each other while the new arrival usually knows very few.

It was a particularly busy time when I arrived in 1964, because a new Labour Government under Harold Wilson's leadership had been elected with a small majority and there was all the excitement of new Ministers being appointed and the inevitable arguments about whether the then Conservative leader, Alec Douglas Home, should be replaced after the election defeat.

So it is little wonder that nobody spoke to me at all on my first day with the exception of a burly chap who tapped me on the shoulder, asking if I was "Taylor", which made me feel that I was right back at school.

He explained that I would feel very lonely, very lost and rather strange in the new situation but counselled me that the whips were the right people to take advice from and that my first task was to give him my address in London. This having been done, I was soon to discover the efficiency of the system, because an envelope arrived marked "from the Chief Whip – Secret", which made me immediately hide it from all those who were having breakfast with

Parliamentary Election—15th October, 1964
CATHCART CONSTITUENCY

vote for
EDWARD M. TAYLOR
the UNIONIST Candidate

1964, October

To the Electors of Cathcart

74 Craig Road,
Glasgow, S.4.
October, 1964.

LADIES AND GENTLEMEN,

In February of this year I was selected by the Cathcart Unionist Association to be the Unionist Candidate for the Division and, now that the election is upon us, I am writing to ask for your support and vote on 15th October.

This is a vital election. Upon its result will depend whether Great Britain will continue to advance along the paths of prosperity and social justice which Unionist Government has made possible, or whether our future will be stifled by the dreary policies and doctrines of the Labour Party which have failed so miserably in the past.

Many issues will be discussed during the campaign but I believe that the most significant will be the question of peace and security. Nobody can now deny that our Government and nation has made a great contribution to world peace. We have adopted a balanced policy of strength and conciliation. Strength to stop wars before they start and conciliation to reach agreement with the Communist Bloc and others who threaten world peace. We reject the idea of giving up our nuclear weapons because, in a dangerous world, to do so would be of no avail. The Britain my Party stands for is not one which will abdicate its international responsibilities or cower under the protection of the United States or any other power. Our voice does count at the International Conference tables, and I believe that this is one of the best guarantees of peace.

In 13 years of Conservative rule, Britain's standard of living has risen more than in the previous half century. We set ourselves a target of doubling our standard of living in 25 years and we are ahead of schedule. From our increased wealth, we have expanded opportunities for the young, provided more generously for the sick, the aged and the unemployed, and have given vast sums in aid towards relieving poverty in the world. This progress can continue and accelerate with Unionist Government.

In Scotland, the basis of a vital new economy has been laid, and will provide the answer to our nation's traditional problem of over-dependence on heavy industry. As a Member of Parliament for Cathcart, I would consider it my duty to see that the claims of Scotland in general and Glasgow in particular continue to receive special attention.

It is no easy task for a young man to comprehend fully the magnitude of responsibility and trust borne by a Member of our British Parliament, but I can promise that, if elected, I shall faithfully and honestly endeavour to uphold, on your behalf, the principles and policies upon which the great achievements and challenging future of our nation depend.

Yours sincerely,

EDWARD M. TAYLOR

1964, October

Points from the MANIFESTO

Top of the League

SOME TORY GOALS

Socialists seem to take pleasure in miscalling our record, but what are the facts ?

EMPLOYMENT LEAGUE. Britain has a better post-war record in maintaining full employment than **any other industrial** nation.

COST LEAGUE. Since 1958, the cost of living has risen less in Britain than in any other European country.

HEALTH LEAGUE. We have the most comprehensive health service in the world, and it is being further improved.

RESEARCH LEAGUE. Britain spends more in research per head than France and West Germany put together.

EDUCATION LEAGUE. We spend a higher proportion of our national income on Education than any other Western European nation.

LIVING STANDARD LEAGUE. The standard of living in Britain is the highest in Europe apart from Sweden.

HELP LEAGUE. Apart from the U.S.A., Britain is the largest contributor to the United Nations. Our record in helping poor and under-developed nations is among the best.

PEACE LEAGUE. Britain's work for peace and disarmament has been second to none. The late President Kennedy paid tribute to our ' indispensible role ' in negotiating the Test Ban Treaty.

KEEP BRITAIN TOP OF THE LEAGUE WITH THE TORIES

Rating Reform

NEED FOR A CHANGE

We all know the faults and injustices of the rating system. In some areas, the increases in rates are outpacing the capacity of householders to pay. Glasgow is one clear example.

The Unionist Party recognises that a reform of rates is required. The method of reform will be determined so soon as the full enquiries (now in progress) are completed. These inquiries cover the whole rating system, potential sources of local government income, the impact of rates now, and Government grants. In carrying out our reforms, we shall bear specially in mind those householders living on small fixed incomes.

Pensions and Politics

THE TORY PLEDGE

Under the Socialists prices soared, but the 26s. pension rose by only 4s. to most, but not all pensioners.

Under the Tories there have been five pension increases and the single person's pension is now £3 7s. 6d. Since 1951 pensions have risen faster than average earnings and much more than the percentage rise in prices. Retirement and widow pensioners can now earn £5 per week **net** with no reduction in pension. Widowed mothers can earn £7 per week net without reduction compared with only £3 in 1951. The Tory pledge for the future is that pensioners and others receiving social security benefits will continue to share in the higher standards produced by an expanding economy. We further pledge that when next we make a general increase in benefits, **preferential treatment will be given to the older pensioners.**

And remember, the Unionists keep their promises.

Taking the High Road

A THOUSAND MILES OF MOTORWAYS

Since 1959, a £600 million programme of road-building has been carried out. During the next five years £1,250 millions will be devoted to this purpose. On our present plans, a thousand miles of motorways will be completed by 1973—in addition we shall improve hundreds of miles of trunk roads and shall concentrate on measures to increase safety.

In Scotland we are constructing a system of dual carriageways linking the main centres from Dundee and Perth through the main industrial areas—Glasgow, Stirling, Fife and Edinburgh. 160 miles of dual carriageway have been completed—double the mileage of four years ago. **In 1963 the Clyde was crossed by tunnel, in 1964 the Forth was spanned by road bridge, and by 1966 the Tay Road Bridge will be built. Top priority now is the High Level Bridge at Erskine.**

Let the Unionists

get on with the job!

1964, October

to the few who don't know him

Glasgow Newspaperman MALCOLM NICOLSON of the *EVENING TIMES*
Interviews EDWARD TAYLOR

You are known throughout Cathcart as Teddy, but what is your full name ?
Edward Macmillan Taylor.

Why Macmillan ?
My grandmother's maiden name was Macmillan. She came from Whiting Bay in Arran, where I still spend most of my holidays.

What age are you ? Married ?
I am 27, and not yet married.

What is your job ?
I am employed by the Clyde Shipbuilding firms, and take part in negotiations with Employers and the Unions on industrial disputes and problems.

Where were you educated ?
The High School of Glasgow and then Glasgow University. My real education, however, started when I joined the Glasgow Town Council !

Mr. Taylor, you became a councillor for Cathcart in January, 1960, but before that you unsuccessfully fought Townhead once and Cowlairs twice. Have you tried to become an M.P. before ?
Yes. Last General Election, in 1959, I was the Tory candidate in Springburn.

Do you think that your Town Council experience would help in Parliament ?
Certainly. Most of the laws made in Westminster are actually carried out by Local Government.

Are you happy with the present Local Government " Set up ? "
No. I think that the present boundaries are out of date. For example, Glasgow cannot deal effectively with its housing and planning problems without a boundary extension.
In addition, the rating system is terribly unjust—we see the worst effects of this in Glasgow.

Why are you a Tory when so many young people lean Left ?
I find that the great majority of young people to-day find that Labour's policies are out of touch with 20th century realities ; and more and more of them are turning towards my Party.

I am a Tory because I believe that a Conservative Government will provide the best opportunity for all people to achieve increased prosperity and security. The Tories have also played a real part in working for World Peace and have ensured that Britain's voice counts in international affairs.

Do your political and Town Council activities leave any time for hobbies ?
Not much, but my hobbies are golf, music and gardening. I am also in the Territorial Army.

How do you normally spend your week-ends ?
On Saturdays—Golf in the morning and football (spectator only) in the afternoon. On Sundays I usually spend the morning doing Corporation correspondence, Sunday School in the afternoon (where I play the piano), church at night and then I usually go visiting friends.

How do you assess your chances in Cathcart, and the Tories generally ?
I think that we can win Cathcart but it will be a tough fight. The Tories will, I think, win the General Election with a good working majority of between 50 and 60.

If you win, what is your ambition ?
To help to make Britain a country which young people will not have to go abroad to seek opportunity, where the aged share in national prosperity, and where family life is based on the security which Peace and Prosperity alone can bring.

1964, October

86

Where to hear Edward Taylor:—

Edward Taylor and other prominent speakers will address the following final meetings. Your questions will be welcomed at all these meetings **except** the Couper Institute Rally on 14th October, at which time will not permit.

FRIDAY, 9th OCTOBER
QUEEN'S PARK SECONDARY, at 7.30 p.m.

MONDAY, 12th OCTOBER
KING'S PARK SECONDARY, at 8.30 p.m.

TUESDAY, 13th OCTOBER
ST. MARGARET MARY'S SECONDARY, at 7.30 p.m.

WEDNESDAY, 14th OCTOBER
DIXON HALLS at 7 p.m.
COUPER INSTITUTE at 8 p.m.

OTHER MEETINGS AS ADVERTISED

Where to help Edward Taylor:—

CENTRAL COMMITTEE ROOMS:
30 CLINCART ROAD, MOUNT FLORIDA (LAN 4244)
Mr. DAVID GOW in charge

Transport - Mr. WM. DUNLOP	Publicity - Mr. GRAHAM SPENCE
Meetings - Mrs. T. L. POTTER, M.B.E.	Postal Votes - Mr. IAN LEITCH
Canvassing - Mr. D. McCULLOCH	Administration - Mrs. ANDERSON

Mount Florida Campaign — Mr. JAMES ANDERSON

CATHCART UNIONIST ROOMS

20 Craig Road
(MER 0044)

Mr. David McKellar in charge

CROSSHILL UNIONIST ROOMS
42 Queen Mary Avenue
(POL 2893)

Cllr. A. Wylie in charge

CROFTFOOT (Temporary) ROOMS
78 Crofthill Road

Mr. A. Galbraith in charge

GOVANHILL PROGRESSIVE ROOMS

21 Belleisle Street

Cllr. J. G. Rennie in charge

CASTLEMILK (Temporary) ROOMS
"The Hut"
Croftfoot Road/Castlemilk Road

Cllr. J. Richmond and Mrs. Q. Knox
in charge

In addition, other temporary rooms will be established in Simshill and Castlemilk

WHERE TO VOTE on THURSDAY, 15th OCTOBER

An official poll card, indicating your polling station and your electoral number, will be sent to you by the returning officer.

(Hours of Polling — 7 a.m. to 9 p.m.)

Published by David Gow, Esq., 30 Clincart Road, Glasgow, S.2.
Printed by C. L. Wright Ltd., 100 West George Street, C.2.

1964, October

CATHCART COMMENTS

MANNY WELEMAN, Cafe Proprietor, of Bogton Avenue, says :
"*We need more young people with ability in Parliament.*"

Mrs. McKENDRICK, Housewife, of Clarkston Road, says :
"*Mr. Taylor has fought well for Cathcart in George Square. Let's give him the same chance at Westminster.*"

GERALD KAVANAGH, Metal Worker of Stravanan Road, says :
"*Castlemilk trusts Taylor—he'll get my vote again.*"

WM. SHEARER, Builder, of Crosshill, says :
"*Socialist leaders like Socialist policies are wild and irresponsible. I'll do my best to keep them out.*"

Mrs. POTTER, M.B.E., of Corrour Road, says :
"*Conservative leadership has brought a real prospect of peace with security.*"

JAMES EWING, Butcher, of Fairfax Avenue, says :
"*We are really moving now on much needed roadworks. Only the Tories will keep up the pace.*"

GEO. DALLAS, of Croftend Avenue, says :
"*Business men know that Socialist policy means Nationalisation, restrictions and needless controls.*"

HUGH McLARTY, O.A.P., Dunagoil Road, says :
"*Councillor Taylor has been a good friend to Cathcart O.A.P.'s He'll get my vote.*"

Mrs. KNOX, of Ardencraig Quadrant, says :
"*All housewives know that Tory policy means a better life for all.*"

Mrs. ROSS, Young Married Housewife, of Boyd Street, says :
"*This is my very first vote—and it's Taylor for me.*"

Miss NANKIVELL, School Teacher, of Menock Road, says :
"*All my friends in King's Park are looking forward to seeing Teddy in action at Westminster.*"

BOB DUNCAN, Salesman, Birgidale Road says :
"*Ted and I serve in the same T.A. unit—I know he'll make a good M.P.*"

1964, October

me in Mrs Fair's guest-house. When I opened the envelope, I found the three sheets of paper which each MP gets every week and which give them a very clear idea of what goes on in Parliament and how back-benchers can operate.

The first sheet is the Party Whip. This is the advice (some say instruction) from the Party Whips on when MPs should attend and how they should vote. In theory, it is simply an invitation to attend, but in practice, it is an indication of what advice the Cabinet or Shadow Cabinet are giving on voting after a private discussion they have had on the issues.

Some days, after explanations of what business is, there are printed the words "Your attendance is requested" with one black line under this latter piece of advice. That is a "One Line Whip". On other days, the description of the business is followed by the words "Your attendance is essential unless you have registered a firm pair", with two black lines underneath. That is the "Two Line Whip". On other days, the description of business is followed with the words "Your attendance is essential" with three black lines. That is the Three Line Whip.

When I first received a Whip, it seemed that there was to be no time off at all, but of course, after a while I learned that the Whip had its own code.

A One Line Whip means that, so far as the Party leadership is concerned, you do not have to attend at all.

A Two Line Whip means that you can absent yourself if you can find someone in the other Party who will agree to absent himself at the same time – this is called a "pair".

A Three Line Whip means that attendance is essential unless the Chief Whip has personally approved absence. Now, of course, this is simply the advice of the Whips and has no statutory or legal authority, but the Party Whips can exert a considerable degree of informal pressure on back-benchers and total pressure on Ministers or Parliamentary spokesman.

A back-bencher who votes against his Party, particularly on an important or sensitive issue, knows that the Whips can hit back in a number of ways.

First, an "unreliable" MP is unlikely to be recommended for office. A few "rebellions" on minor issues, or on issues where the member has clearly established personal views, can be disregarded, but a member who appears to just go his own way and vote on his feelings of the day, or to criticise with his vote some fundamental features of government policy is unlikely to make progress in the Parliamentary ladder unless there is a change of leadership – and even then "unreliable" people are rarely rewarded. The Whips react strongest against those who ignore Whips to support "popular" causes, because members doing this are believed not only to make the Government's defence more difficult, but also cause embarrassment to their colleagues in other constituencies.

The second deterrent which the Whips have, is that they control the whole area of patronage. They recommend people for important committees, for "trips" or deputations abroad, for "special leave of absence" and for honours. In short, a well-behaved MP is more likely to get a favour when he wants it than one who goes his own way.

The third, and most serious deterrent, is that the Whips can, through the Party machine, report back to constituency parties that the member has been "letting the side down" and this could lead to the member perhaps not being selected to fight the next election. These are broad generalisations. Some MPs who have rebelled have broken through to high office. Others who have been 100 per cent Party supporters get nowhere at all.

The deterrents I have mentioned, though, are a fair summary of the Whips' power, but what this means, of course, is that if an MP, is not anxious to secure promotion (or has given up hope), does not want to go on a "fact finding mission" to the Bahamas or Brazil, and has the full support from his constituency party for what he is doing, the power of the Whips over him is minimal.

So how should an MP actually vote on issues? It is a really perplexing problem for many.

Some would argue that he should vote for what he thinks is right in every case, in every Bill and on every amendment. Others argue that his duty is to vote as he thinks his constituents believe at the time. Others argue that his duty is invariably to support his party under whose banner he was elected. All these arguments have their defects and the right answer lies somewhere in between. There are obviously no circumstances in which an MP should vote for something in Parliament which he believes to be wholly against the interests of the nation – because if he did, there would be no point in going to Parliament at all – a voting machine could do the same job. On the other hand, an MP should not ignore the fact that he has a duty to support his party. Likewise an MP has a clear duty to have regard for the wishes of constituents in his voting, but at the same time his main obligation to voters is to use his judgement as best he can in the long-term interests of his voters. I think the greatest crime for an MP is to vote for a policy which is apparently "popular" as a means of seeking personal support if he knows that the policy in question is impractical and unjust.

MPs do, from time to time, go through agonies in deciding where there duty lies. For me, the biggest problem came in 1971 when I was a Junior Minister in Ted Heath's Government, and when Mr Heath put a Motion before Parliament to support Britain joining the Common Market.

On the one hand, it was obvious that EEC membership was the clear policy of the Party and that I had an obligation to it. Likewise, it was pretty clear that the majority of my constituents and certainly those who voted for me, were in favour of membership at that time. In addition, I knew that to vote against the EEC would mean resigning my post in the Government and presumably thereafter being unable to devote what talents I believed I had in the interests of the UK, in a position of authority in government.

But on the other hand, I was wholly convinced, despite many discussions with colleagues and a long personal chat with Ted Heath himself, that joining the EEC would be a recipe, in the long term, for the undermining of democracy. Britain would become a peripheral part of an area in structural decline. We would undermine the special relationship which Britain had with the Commonwealth and the USA and we would deprive future British Governments of freedom of action in many areas of policy. The EFTA grouping seemed to me to be an ideal association with Europe which did not involve surrenders of sovereignty, bureaucratic legislation and policies or the undermining of our links with the growth areas of the world. As a candidate I had found myself in full agreement with the papers published by the Foreign Secretary, Reggie Maudling, which had supported EFTA but had explained why Britain could not become a full member of the EEC.

After much thought, to the annoyance of some of my local party, I resigned my post, voted against the Government and joined the ranks of the anti-marketeers.

The dilemma I had was the same dilemma which many MPs and many junior and senior Ministers have to face up to. The only general guidance which one can give to any new MP is that before voting one way or another he should ask himself the simple question of why he is inclined to vote in a particular way. If the answer is popularity, self-interest or spite, he will know he is wrong. It is the motive rather than the issue which is the real test.

The winning team celebrating the result of a Glasgow Cathcart Parliamentary Election, with my agent, Jimmy Anderson (in glasses)

10

How Westminster works

The second piece of paper which was delivered in the Chief Whip's "secret" communication was the summary of Party Committees and it gives a real clue as to how MPs seek to influence government decisions or the decisions on policy of the opposition parties. Each week, there used to be 30 Conservative Committee meetings in the Rooms upstairs in the Commons on the floor above the Commons Chamber and every policy area was covered. For example, on a normal Tuesday, there were meetings of the Foreign Affairs Committee and Committees on Health, Trade, Agriculture, Media, Urban Affairs, Aviation, Finance and Wales.

Looking down the list of Committees, I suggested politely to my friendly whip on my second day that perhaps I might be considered for any vacancy on the Shipbuilding Committee and the Scottish Committee in due course, but he responded by telling me that I was a member of all the committees!

It seems ridiculous when you consider that four separate committees meet at 5pm on a Tuesday, but strange to say, this is how the system worked.

Every Conservative MP is entitled to attend every single committee. This is our vehicle for letting off steam in private on subjects, and as each committee has office bearers and a whip in attendance, the conclusions of each committee are faithfully reported by the office bearers to the Minister or Shadow Minister covering the subject and the whips will report the conclusions to the Chief Whip. Of course, a similar procedure applies to the Labour Party.

Apart from being a way in which members can

homes for scotland

Homes for Scotland have high priority in Tory plans. Labour has failed to build at the rate needed. In 1965 only 35,116 keys to completed houses were handed over compared with 37,171 in 1964. Council building dropped by 2,991.

Ayrshire built 207 fewer houses, Glasgow dropped nearly 5% and in Kilmarnock the 69 houses built in 1964 were followed by only 29 in 1965.

Tory plans will remove slums from the Scottish scene. They will encourage the use of modern techniques and really help local authorities who need the houses. A sensible housing policy is essential for the mobility of labour that a modern Scottish economy needs, and with

the new houses will go a scheme for fair council rents linked with rebate schemes.

Private property for renting will be expanded by depreciation allowances for buildings and emphasis on housing societies. Rents for private houses will be frozen in districts with a housing shortage.

Private ownership wherever possible is Tory

policy. Assistance will be given to people who want to own their own houses. Many find it a struggle to put down the deposit. Tory plans will help by grants related to the savings people have made by themselves. And for those who do not receive full mortgage tax relief, the Tories will provide help through the building societies.

Government sponsored research on building techniques will be expanded and higher standards of architecture and construction will be encouraged. The Tories will act to give a private owner redress for poor quality in a new house.

Tory plans will get good housing where it is needed for the people who want it.

The Housing Need !

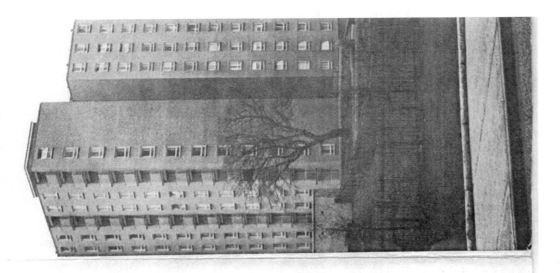

On THURSDAY, 31st MARCH, 1966

VOTE

EDWARD TAYLOR

Published by James Anderson, Election Agent, 30 Clincart Road, Glasgow, S.2.
Printed by Thorams, 42 & 46 Holmlea Road, Glasgow, S.4.

Published by the Scottish Unionist Association, 11 Atholl Crescent, Edinburgh, 3

Printed by Thomas Nason (Printers) Ltd., Parkside Works, Edinburgh, 9

vote conservative

1966, March

let off steam and fire warning shots against the bows of Ministries about policies, the committees are also a source of information for MPs and a link between the Party groups and outside bodies. For example, the Home Affairs Committee holds regular meetings at which bodies like the Police Federation, the Prison Affairs Association, the Probation Officers and the wide range of organisations concerned with home affairs matters can make their views clear to backbench MPs and through the back-benchers to the party leaders. Attendance at the normal committee meetings tend to vary between 20 to 40 with the "regulars" being those with a special interest in the subject, but when some big issue arises, the MPs crowd in the meeting to let their views be known.

I can think of three meetings of Party Committees which had a vital role in decision-making.

First, we had the meeting of the European Committee when Sir Keith Joseph appeared to justify his plans to cut student grants for youngsters coming from middle income homes and to charge fees for tuition. The members present gave him such a rough ride that it became clear that the plans might spark off a major Commons revolt in the Chamber. So, shortly after the meeting, it was announced that the plans had been drastically changed.

Even more electric was the meeting of the Foreign Affairs Committee which took place just after the invasion of the Falkland Isles by the Argentinians. There was a widespread view amongst the back-benchers, that the Foreign Office – never too popular amongst Conservatives – had let Britain down, first by making decisions which might encourage the Argentinians to believe that Britain would not resist an invasion, and second by failing to provide intelligence about the invasion build up. There was even a belief amongst some that the Foreign Office was keen to ditch the Falkland Islands and thereby remove a constant source of irritation in our relations with Southern American states. So when the Foreign Secretary, Lord Carrington, appeared before the Committee, he was heckled and even abused. Within hours, Lord Carrington came to the conclusion that he did not have the confidence of the Parliamentary Party and tendered his resignation. Backbench power, which is rarely used in such a dramatic way, had shown its punch. There was something rather similar, although clouded with a bit of mystery, when we had the meeting of the 1922 Committee – the back-benchers weekly meeting which most attend – at which Leon Brittan's role in the Westland dispute was discussed. The majority of those who spoke, including some respected and normally loyal MPs, suggested that Mr Brittan had caused embarrassment to the Party and should resign. He did indeed resign within a few days although I was never quite sure whether the 1922 meeting was the main motivating factor. However, Leon did indicate in his resignation statement that the loss of confidence of the back-benchers had been a principal motivation in his decision.

So the Party Committees are not just meaningless consultation. They can influence policies quite considerably although in a less dramatic way than the three examples I have quoted above, and the Committees do play a vital role if any groups of MPs wish to pursue a particular campaign.

Apart from these official Party Committees, there are also the secret dining clubs where MPs discuss issues in private and act as a kind of self-help group to promote the election of their members to Party Committee office bearer posts. These posts are quite important, as the election of people with particular views can often influence the advice given to the Party and also the media presentation of Party opinion. For example, if there is a big row about a defence issue, the BBC and other media groups tend to interview and seek advice from office bearers of the Defence Committee.

Shortly after I went to the Commons, I was invited to join the very secret "92" group which consists of what is generally regarded as the right wing back-benchers. Its very existence was a total secret for many years although its secrecy was blown during a Party crisis when a clever Times reporter parked outside the Club where we were meeting for one of our regular dinners and discussions and proceeded to publish the names. A comparable group of the mainly left of centre Conservatives has been in operation also for many years. Having mentioned the Party Committees, it would be wrong not to mention the many All Party Committees which exist in Parliament. These are again official groups, but tend to bring MPs who meet together to promote or to study issues of common concern. There is, for example, a temperance all party group of MPs who meet together to promote temperance and to battle against legislation which might appear to encourage the consumption of alcohol. There is an All Party Penal Reform Group, a Committee on the Chemical Industry, on Drug Abuse, on Management, on Scientific Affairs and on the Retail Trade plus a host of bodies taking an interest in particular foreign countries. My experience is that few of these all party committees have a vital impact on decision making, but they do provide a most useful link between MPs and outside organisations.

But MPs do not spend all their time seeking to influence policy. A lot of the work is humdrum and repetitive. Perhaps we can get the best picture by going through an average day for a reasonably conscientious MP

The day normally starts with the MP arriving around 9.30am to do two tasks. First he must reply to his daily bundle of letters and second he must read through the Parliamentary papers.

Most MPs have a secretary working at the House of Commons and the MP will either dictate his mail or give guidance to the secretary about how it should be dealt with. MPs receive a lot of letters although the busier MPs with a higher profile in the public eye tend to get a lot more. They can be on many subjects.

Most of the letters relate to grievances or requests for help. They relate to direct issues of Ministerial or departmental responsibility, or to the affairs of local councils. If someone feels that he is not receiving adequate assistance from say, the Ministry of Health and Social Services, he may write to his MP who will take up the issues with the department or the local office of the Ministry. Likewise on tax affairs, immigration, education, student grants, housing allocations, planning applications and so on. A normal daily mail-bag might contain about twenty such requests. Then there are those offering views on policies – with much of this mail coming from local firms and organisations. Then there are the invitations – to attend constituency functions, lunches or seminars promoted by the many bodies seeking to influence policy, and of course there are the many circulars from industrial concerns and public relations bodies, many of which tend to end up in the wastepaper baskets.

An MP normally pursues requests for help from constituents most assiduously, because the MP is the only person with a direct access to Ministers and Departments and many grievances are resolved that way. Often an explanation in writing from a Minister can satisfy an enquirer who before then only had the advice of a junior official in his local office. This is all an essential part of our democracy.

After the mail, the Parliamentary papers have to be studied, and this can be a tough job, because so many of the Parliamentary papers are complicated and almost meaningless to the MP without specialist knowledge.

These papers fall into six broad categories ... Hansard, Order Paper, Bills, Regulations, White Papers and Papers of other colours.

Hansard is a remarkable document. MPs receive it about 9am and it records every word in the previous days sitting in the debates at least up till 10pm. Not only is every word of every speech recorded, but even every interruption and heckle. Even nods of the head are recorded. For example, if an MP is speaking whom I might disagree with and I shout out "rubbish", the Hansard reporters would faithfully record in the text "Mr Teddy Taylor (Southend East) "Rubbish!" If another is speaking whom I agree with and nod my head, the clever reporters in the gallery would record, if they thought it significant, "Mr Teddy Taylor indicated assent."

But why do MPs bother reading Hansard if they have heard the debates the previous day? The answer is that they may not have been present all the time and even if they were present, they may wish to check up on what was actually said. However, the main reason for the morning "read" is to look at the long list of written answers to questions. While some Parliamentary questions are actually asked, the great majority are written ones, and the Ministerial answers are one of the main sources of information for MPs. If say, a Minister publishes a table of statistics about, for example, regional rates of unemployment, the pattern of road accidents, the costs of agricultural support, or even on the delays in Defence Ministry contracts, MPs might be able to identify worrying or encouraging trends and to use them to pursue issues through the Parliamentary mechanism. Hansard is also a tool which MPs use as a means of correcting or drawing attention to shifts in government policy. For example, if a Prime Minister is arguing that he or she is achieving success in keeping the value of the currency stable in international markets, it can be acutely embarrassing to have an MP reading from Hansard a statement in the previous session when the same Prime Minister might have argued that it was the government's policy to let the currency find its own level in international markets. Nothing upsets MPs and Ministers more than to be charged with inconsistency.

Next we have the Order Paper. This is the MPs guide to the business of the day. It records first the list of oral questions which are to be asked that day and an MP who had perhaps been advised that morning of the closure of a local textile firm might observe that another had a question to the Industry Minister about the future of the textile industry. He would obviously wish to be present in the House and to seek to use the other question as a means of drawing the Government's attention to the problem in the constituency. In addition to the list of questions, the Order Paper records the division lists of the previous nights debate and, perhaps more important, the list of questions which MPs have tabled for answer in future days.

There is also a list of "Parliamentary motions" – a device which MPs use to draw attention to issues of concern and to rally support. These motions are never debated, but are simply used as a means of recording points of view. For example, if an MP is anxious to persuade the Government to take further steps against drunken drivers, through a policy of permitting random breath tests, he might well table a Motion in the following terms which would be printed in the following day's Order Paper:-

"That this House is alarmed by the sharp increase in the incidence of drunken driving and calls upon H.M.Government to authorise the police to carry out random breath tests."

Once the Motion is published, two things normally happen. First the details of the Motion might be highlighted in the Press and TV and the MPs of all parties who agree with the sentiment will go into the Table Office and sign the Motion. Each day, the numbers of MPs who have supported the Motion are published in the Order Paper. If the Motion attracts, say, only a dozen signatures, the issue is likely to die a death. But if, say, 100 MPs sign, this would be an indication to the Party Whips of a strong opinion in Parliament and Ministers would start asking their civil servants if the idea was practical. They might also, if the Department disagreed fundamentally with the issue, seek Parliamentary opportunities to put the converse case. But an MP whose Motion attracted 100 names might be encouraged to pursue his issues through Parliamentary questions, discussions at Party Committees or even by promoting a Private Members Bill.

In fairness, Motions are often used for blatant political or self-promotion purposes. If an MP moves a Motion calling upon the Government to provide extra aid to the shipbuilding industry, it might look quite splendid in local papers if the MP represents a shipbuilding area, and the local constituents, being unaware of the workings of Parliament, might gain the impression that their MP had initiated a really significant Parliamentary move to assist them.

Bills flow constantly through the Commons and there are three types of bills. First we have the bills promoted by the Government which, because they follow a long period of consultation, are usually almost certain to become law. Then you have Private Member's Bills. These bills are many and varied, but are unlikely to ever become law unless the MP has been successful in drawing a high place in the private members' ballot or unless they are thoroughly uncontroversial. Even those at the top of the list are unlikely to be successful in making their bills law if there is significant opposition to them, unless the Government is prepared to allow additional time for their debate. Without such time, a hard core of opponents can "filibuster" a Private Member's Bill until the limited discussion time is exhausted. A good example of this, was Enoch Powell's Bill of 1985 called the Unborn Children (Protection) Bill, which was designed to ban experimentation in embryos. It was passed with a huge Commons majority, but fell by the wayside because a small band of opponents talked it into the ground and the Government was unwilling to make more time available for it. On the other hand, David Steel's much earlier Abortion Bill, although again opposed by the vociferous minority, did become law because the Government of the day allowed extra time.

The third category of bills is the Private Bills. Public Bills have to apply to everyone – but a Private Bill, which is usually promoted by a local authority or public body like a Harbour Board, tends to apply only to a special area. For example, a bill which gives all harbour authorities the right to charge higher fees on vessels coming into their harbour, would be a Public Bill, but a bill giving the power only to the Mersey Docks and Harbour Board would be a Private Bill. There is also a form of bill which is both private and public called a Hybrid Bill, which involves the most complex of procedures. This is the form of legislation which is required to facilitate the legislation on the Channel Tunnel.

But how do MPs gather all the information which is necessary to make objective judgements on the complicated bills and how do they assess how new bills might affect their constituencies or national interests which they may be worried about?

The answer is that MPs cannot master every subject, but they must build up a reliable network of professional advice. To give just one example, I was a bit lost myself when put on the Committee to debate, in detail, a rather difficult bill called the Data Protection Bill which introduced restrictions on the publicising of material in computer data banks. My immediate reaction was to send off the bill to a number of local bodies, including the giant Access Company, to seek their views on the bill together with any suggestions for change.

The same rules apply to the multitude of regulations which come before Parliament. These are "mini-laws" which deal with detailed issues. For example, a Public Bill on agriculture might give the Secretary of State the power, whenever he chooses, to ban the use of particular chemicals or hormones in agricultural production. So we might have, for example, the Nitrate Fertiliser Regulations being issued by Government banning the use of such chemicals. The regulations, unlike bills, do not go through a long and complicated procedure, but usually end up, if controversial, with a debate of one and a half hours after 10pm.

But the regulations can have dynamic consequences. For example, when the Government proposed, in a regulation, tight flying control on flying objects, a phone call to my local factory producing advertising balloons showed that the regulations, if enacted, could put them and their workers out of business. All of which necessitated urgent contacts with Ministers happily resulting in the rules being changed. Likewise, a minor order, under a law on safe toys, which proposed a ban on scented erasers, was sent to a local distributor of fancy goods who responded that he had £100,000 of the erasers in stock and would face ruin if the regulations went through. We had a fierce battle in Parliament, in the course of which, I was able to stir up a lot of backbench support. Sadly, the regulation was eventually forced through and the only thing I was able to secure for my constituent firm, was a delay in application.

Watching laws and regulations is a vital part of an MPs work and if he lets something slip through Parliament, which causes great damage to a local firm or a group of constituents, he is obviously letting them down. The MP is their watchdog and must do his job.

Then there are White Papers. These are not laws, but tend to set out the policy or laws which the Government intends to pursue in particular areas. For example, there might be a White Paper published on Drug Abuse which would set out a range of new measures which the Government plans to introduce. Apart from informing the public of Government intentions, the White Paper also gives an opportunity for MPs and outside bodies to make representations on the desirability of changes of policy before the proposed laws are actually published or drafted.

A Green Paper is rather different, because instead of setting out the Government's intentions, it sets out the Government's desire to "do something" about a problem and lists the various solutions which might be adopted, giving details of the possible consequences of each alternative. The idea of a Green Paper is to concentrate the minds of MPs and outside bodies and to give them the opportunity of saying which option they would prefer. For example, a Green Paper on Rating Reform went through the various options like a local income tax, a sales tax, a poll tax and hypothecated national revenue.

There are also a lot of Blue Papers – and the most important of these are the reports of select committees of MPs who have been appointed to monitor policy in particular areas. For example, the Trade and Industry Select Committee, which like all select committees has the power to summon witnesses and demand information from them, looked with care into the question of Britain's growing imbalance of trade in manufactures with the EEC, and their report put all the facts and arguments plus possible remedies to Parliament as a whole. There are also Red Papers which usually relate to the work of the Treasury with their income and expenditure forecasts and Budget proposals. Like almost every activity these days, the flow of paper through Parliament continues to grow and one of the major tasks of MPs is to keep abreast of it all and to ensure that they have a proper idea of the subjects, so that they can protect constituents and advance their various crusades.

How does the sifting work, in practice, for the busy MPs? Say we take a hypothetical London MP looking at his daily papers. A regulation on Welsh land drainage? Probably straight into the bucket! A regulation on the disposal of chemical waste? It looks complicated, but there's a local factory which produces some chemical things, so it should be sent off to the manager with a request for his assessment of how it would affect his factory, if implemented. A regulation on DHSS benefits for people living in bed and breakfast accommodation? There are lots of homeless people in London, so perhaps it should be sent for comment to organisations helping the homeless. A regulation on aids for disabled people? The MP may have championed the cause of the disabled, so will wish to study this himself in detail. A bill on Capital Gains Tax liability? Perhaps put it aside to be looked at when there is time. If it means more concessions for those with large assets, it might provide an opportunity for a political attack on the Government. A bill on animal welfare? Oh dear – just the kind of thing to spark off lots of letters from constituents, so better to find out what's being proposed. A letter to the Agricultural Minister might be appropriate to get an idea in a short letter of what the problem is and what the Government is trying to do.

A Private Members Bill on the registration of plumbers? Looks fairly innocuous, but as the person promoting the Bill is Joe Bloggs, who is a friend, perhaps it would be best to speak to him in the lobby to-night just in case it might affect local plumbers.

A White Paper on drug abuse? White Papers are usually more easy to understand than bills because they are not couched in legal language. Like most other MPs, our London friend would probably read at least the summary of proposals and, if the summary looks interesting or unusual, the full text may be read. A Green Paper on housing benefit? This could be big stuff and could be a prelude to the Government seeking to change the whole system which could have a major impact on elderly constituents. Probably it would be wise to go to the Social Services Committee meeting of the Party next week where it will no doubt be referred to and debated.

A Red Paper on public expenditure? A quick read would be justified as it will probably give a clue as to whether the next budget is likely to be good or bad.

A Private Bill on the Docklands Railway? Oh dear – these things usually give powers to acquire property, to build new roads and to upset life for constituents. Better send a letter to British Rail to ask specifically how the Bill might affect the residents and industries in his constituency.

A Private Members' Bill on the protection of caterpillars? Better watch this with all the environmental lobbyists these days. Who is promoting the Bill? Old Reggie Bull? No – he's a bit of a loony and always putting forward daft ideas which Ministers explain is based on duff gen. He was the chap who argued that beetles were being eradicated and then we had the plague of beetles in Newcastle. Into the wastepaper basket with this one.

And so it goes on. MPs have to make quick decisions on the relevance of the mass of paper themselves, but always have to remember the dangers of chucking in the bucket something which might just be of direct relevance to a constituency interest.

Some argue that MPs nowadays can rely on research assistants to do their trawling work, but most researchers are bright young men who just haven't the knowledge or experience to sift through papers of this sort. If they are of that special category, they will probably be moving to a better job very quickly. In practice, almost every MP has to do his own sifting and the buck stops with him!

11

The Parliamentary day

The biggest change that has been made in Parliament in recent times, has been the Blair reform of working hours in Parliament. Until Mr Blair appeared in Downing Street, the Parliamentary week was clear, specific and arduous. The Parliamentary day did not begin officially until 2.30pm and proceeded until at least 10.30pm or midnight, if there was a debate on some regulations. However, on Tuesdays, Thursdays and sometimes Wednesdays, there were meetings of Committees of MPs who had been allocated the task of studying legislation in detail. If the Committees were considering complex or controversial legislation, they were given the authority to meet in mornings, afternoons and evenings as well. These Committees could sometimes be quite horrendous, because attendance meant that not only did the MPs miss vital debates in the House of Commons, but had to sit and endure long discussions on the most complex and detailed aspects of legislation.

Shortly after I arrived in the Commons, I was appointed to the Committee on a Transport Bill being promoted by Barbara Castle. It was highly controversial and as our Party was in Opposition, we were responsible for most of the long sittings.

There was one week we proceeded from a Tuesday morning until Friday lunchtime with total breaks of only about 20 hours. We had two deaths of Committee members during the long sittings and although it would be wrong to attribute their deaths directly to the long sittings, I cannot believe that the strain would have no effect. The strain was particularly great for Ministers who had to run their departments and deal with the constant crises in their fields of activity while the Committee was still sitting.

But why do we have Committees at all? They are certainly a vital part of the consideration given to Bills.

When a Bill is first published, it is reported formally to the House of Commons. This is known as the First Reading of the Bill. At this point, the details of the Bill are available to the general public and in particular, to any organisation which might be affected; and they will take an early opportunity to contact Government Ministers or MPs to let them know of any concerns or enthusiasm for the proposals.

The next stage – usually about a week or two later, is to have a debate in the House of Commons, about the principle of the Bill. The idea of this is that the MPs sit down and debate, not the details of the legislation, but more the principle of whether the proposed law is a good or a bad idea.

MPs debate the Bill on a Monday and Tuesday from about 4pm till 10pm, but from 12.30pm till 7pm, or occasionally 6pm, if the debate takes place on a Wednesday or Thursday. Before the changes, we would have one of the longer debates until 10pm on each day of the week, apart from Friday. At the end of the debate, there is a vote; and if more people vote in the "Ayes" lobby rather than the "Noes" lobby, the Bill will then proceed to the next stage, which is, consideration in detail in a Committee. A group of between 20 and 30 MPs are appointed, in lists determined by the Whips, after consultation with Ministers or Opposition spokesmen and they get down to business in a fortnight or so.

However, for some of the more significant constitutional Bills like EU membership and the

Parliamentary Election — 31st March, 1966
CATHCART CONSTITUENCY

vote for
EDWARD M. TAYLOR
the CONSERVATIVE Candidate

1966, March

OUR PLAN

The Conservatives, if Elected will carry out this Programme

"I am determined to promise nothing that we cannot achieve—I call not for words—but for Actions."—Edward Heath, 5th March, 1966.

A PLEDGE ON RATES

Rates can be reduced by one-tenth. For Glasgow this means about 3/ in the £. This will be achieved by transferring £100 million of rating expenditure to the Exchequer.

We will sweep away the crazy anomalies of the system — such as the rating of night storage and other forms of heating.

JUSTICE IN PENSIONS

The Tory Pension plan is :—

Everyone must have a good pension with their job on top of the State pension.

Pension rights should be preserved despite changes in job.

The earnings rule will be eased.

Pensions will be provided for the " Forgotten Few " who have no N.I. Pensions.

Public Services and Forces Pensions will be reviewed every two years AND maintain their purchasing power.

The thrifty who have put by some savings will be helped by raising the amount disregarded before a supplementary pension is granted.

The age barrier of 50 which deprives some widows of pensions will be reviewed.

Prescription charges will be re-introduced — subject to wide exceptions such as the elderly, chronic sick, disabled, expectant and nursing mothers.

CHALKING UP THE HALF MILLION

Our target is :—

An annual rate of 500,000 homes by the end of 1968.

A crash slum clearance drive in big cities like Glasgow.

A massive increase in houses for the elderly.

BUYING A HOUSE ?

Conservatives will help all home buyers by :—

Sound economic management to ensure lower interest rates for everyone. Grants to help with deposits.

The same tax relief for those on lower incomes as for those paying tax at standard rate.

Exchequer help again for the buying of older houses through the Building Societies.

Giving home buyers a guarantee of good workmanship.

CUT THE TAXES

We will cut the intolerable tax burden. Hard work and enterprise should be fairly rewarded.

Too many feel that extra effort is not worthwhile because of unfair tax rates.

Under the Conservatives income tax was cut 5 times. In one year Labour has increased taxes by £627 millions — about £1 per week more for the average family.

BEAT THE CRIME WAVE

A Conservative Secretary of State would be directly responsible for a determined drive against crime in Scotland.

Many new measures are planned to strengthen the police and to make criminals pay for the injuries and damage they do. More effective means of deterring criminals, particularly young delinquents, will be introduced.

STRIKING A BARGAIN

Unofficial strikes which disrupt industry and cause hardship to the public can and will be dealt with.

Conservatives will :—

1. Make sure that agreements between unions and employers are kept by making them legally enforceable.

2. Establish an Industrial Court to deal with disputes and appeals against unjust dismissals.

3. Introduce measures to deal with restrictive labour practices.

CONSERVATIVE PLANS FOR SCOTLAND ARE BEARING FRUIT NOW

Labour's new investment grant plan means less aid over a much wider area. Conservatives will re-introduce their successful growth point scheme.

We will also :

1. Provide more Government training centres to ease the burden of workers from old industries to new.

2. Restore the cuts which Labour made in road building.

3. Set up inter-city travel by encouraging competition on Scottish air routes.

THE ROAD TO KNOWLEDGE

Our greatest British asset is our young people.

Conservatives will expand educational opportunities for everyone.

The recent cut of 25% of the University Building programme is crazy and short-sighted. This cut will be restored immediately.

There will be a realistic drive for more teachers, measures to enable part-time teachers to qualify for a pension, plus the encouraging of more married women to return to teaching.

OR ACTION

SOARING PRICES

Conservatives cut price increases to an average of 2½% yearly in their last 5 years. Prices soared by 5% in Labour's first year.

Number one priority is to control this spiral which damages the economy and brings hardship to those on fixed incomes.

We will protect housewives against misleading "guarantees" and there will be higher safety standards for food and household goods.

THE CUSTOMER IS RIGHT

Gas, electricity, and railway undertakings have a duty to give consumer service and to deal with complaints speedily and thoroughly.
Conservatives will see that the consumer comes first.

THE KEY TO RHODESIA

Conservatives will break the deadlock by starting talks without strings with Mr. Smith and his colleagues. Object — a constitutional settlement. This is the answer to a problem which could lead to great bloodshed in Africa.

Where to Hear EDWARD TAYLOR

EDWARD TAYLOR and other Prominent Speakers will address the following Final Meetings. Your questions will be answered at all these meetings, except the Couper Institute Rally on 31st March, at which time will not permit.

MONDAY, 28th MARCH

GLENWOOD S.S. SCHOOL at 7 p.m.

ARNPRIOR PRIMARY SCHOOL, at 8 p.m.

TUESDAY, 29th MARCH

KING'S PARK S.S. SCHOOL, at 7 p.m.

KING'S PARK PRIMARY SCHOOL, at 8 p.m.

WEDNESDAY, 30th MARCH

DIXON HALLS, at 7 p.m.

COUPER INSTITUTE, at 8 p.m.

Where to Help EDWARD TAYLOR

Phone or call at

CENTRAL COMMITTEE ROOMS

30 CLINCART ROAD

MOUNT FLORIDA (LAN 4244)

Where to Vote on THURSDAY, 31st MARCH

An official Poll Card, indicating your Polling Station and your Electoral Number, will be sent to you by the Returning Officer.

(Hours of Polling — 7 a.m. to 9 p.m.)

To the Electors of Cathcart Ward

LADIES AND GENTLEMEN,

Eighteen months ago you elected me to be your representative in the House of Commons. Since then I have done my best to represent the interests of the whole Constituency in Parliament and have spoken up in the House on matters which I know that many of you regarded as important. In my short service at Westminster I have been greatly helped by the many Cathcart folk who sent me their views on national problems and messages of support on the points of view I expressed.

Speaking in the House is, of course, only part of an M.P.'s work. One of the main tasks is to deal with constituent's personal problems and complaints of injustice. I have made myself available to constituents each Saturday morning and will certainly continue a regular interview session if I am re-elected on 31st March. I cannot promise to resolve all problems, but can assure you that I will do my best.

In October, 1964, a Labour Government was returned to power after making considerable promises to the electorate. Now it is clear that many of these election pledges were irresponsible and misleading. The programme, we were told, would involve no rise in taxes. In one year, the tax burden has risen by £627 millions. The cost of living would be stabilised—yet prices rose by 5 per cent. in Labour's first year. Promised increases in school building, universities and roads have been replaced by savage cuts. The University building programme, for example, has been cut by a quarter. Despite promised action, rates have soared and the new Rating Bill will simply add to the burden of the great majority of Ratepayers. Mortgage rates have remained at a record figure and even the Government's " death-bed repentance " proposals, to help those on low incomes, is accompanied by renewed talk of yet higher rates of interest. And the minimum income guarantee and half-pay on retirement plans, which were to be amongst the first jobs of a Labour Government, have been indefinitely postponed.

The most serious failure of the Government, however, is the fact that production has been stagnant. Enterprise and initiative have been stifled by high taxes and many young people are being forced to leave the country to look for a fair reward for their efforts.

If production remains stagnant and prices continue to soar there is a very real danger of Britain again being forced to devalue its currency. The answer to this is not to impose more controls, but to set industry free and give the nation's people scope for exercising their talents.

The Conservative answer to the nation's problems is given in our Manifesto and I have summarised in this document the salient points in our programme. The top priorities are to control the prices spiral and to bring taxes down again. By doing these things we can safeguard the nation's currency and also pave the way for real growth and prosperity in the future.

The promises which we make to assist pensioners, ratepayers, owner-occupiers have been carefully costed and can be carried out in a five-year Parliament and still reduce the level of tax. The promises may not be as ambitious as those of other parties, but my Party has a record of keeping its promises and we are determined to offer nothing that cannot be achieved.

I am glad to see that my Party has promised a vigorous drive to beat the crime wave. The statistics of crime are alarming and the Government's duty is to take strong and decisive action. Another promise which will be of special interest to Cathcart residents is the pledge to ensure that consumer service in the nationalised industries will be improved. When great industries like gas and electricity supply have a publicly protected monopoly, it is only right that they should make special efforts to ensure a good service and a speedy investigation of complaints.

I sincerely believe that Labour's short tenure of office has led to the weakening of the economy, the weakening of our defences, and the stifling of the energies of our people. Its promises have proved to be empty ones and Conservative fears have proved to be more than justified.

The Labour answer is more controls. They are pledged to nationalise steel and to bring the aircraft industry into public ownership. In addition, the £150 millions given to the Industrial Re-organisation Corporation can, and probably will be used to achieve the Socialist's declared aim of controlling the commanding heights of the economy.

This policy will not solve the nation's problems, nor will it achieve the progress which, properly led, our nation can make. Only a Conservative Government will re-create a strong and prosperous Britain and I appeal to you to give the Party your support.

May I also say that it has been a very great pleasure to represent this Constituency and I would ask for your support so that I can again fulfil, to the best of my ability, the rather exhausting but immensely satisfying task of the Member of Parliament for Cathcart.

Sincerely yours,

EDWARD TAYLOR

YOUR M.P. AT WORK
(or 24 hours in the life of EDWARD TAYLOR)

The hectic life of an M.P. makes air travel a must.

Here he is arriving from Westminster at Renfrew on a typical Friday evening.

* * *

Constituency functions and meetings occupy Friday nights.

Here he is with three Queen's Scouts at King's Park after their prize giving.

* * *

No long lie on Saturday. It's "Surgery" at 10 o'clock at the Conservative Rooms in Mount Florida.

Over 80 Cathcart folk seek his advice each month at these weekly interview sessions.

Here is a typical " consultation " taking place.

* * *

Home for lunch then around the constituency to discuss problems with those unable to attend the morning " Surgery." This is a grand chance to meet Cathcart folk and hear their views.

Here Taylor is making some new young friends in Castlemilk.

* * *

Early evening — and still on the job. Church Bazaars, Sales of Work and Flower Shows are always happy occasions — the old folk are not forgotten.

Here he is having a chat with pensioners at a Castlemilk function.

Photographs 2 & 5 by kind permission of the *Rutherglen Reformer*.

LABOUR PROMISE	LABOUR PERFORMANCE
Cost of Living ' The constant rise in the cost of living . . . will be halted '. (GEORGE BROWN — *September*, 1964).	Prices up 5 per cent., in Labour's first year — the highest rise for 10 years.
Tax ' Labour will not need to increase taxation to pay for its programme '. (DOUGLAS HOUGHTON — *October*, 1964).	£627 million more tax plus £265 million in N.I. stamps, postal charges and T.V. licence. An extra 24/- per week for the average family.
Homes ' We have pledged ourselves to tackle the housing problem like a wartime operation '. (HAROLD WILSON — *October*, 1964).	More than 2,000 fewer homes in Scotland in 1965.
Mortgages ' We shall cheapen the cost of housing by our interest rate policy '. (HAROLD WILSON). ' What we have in mind is something around 3 per cent '. (GEORGE BROWN — *October*, 1964).	Mortgage rates at the highest ever level, and rumours of a further rise.
Rates ' We shall give early relief to ratepayers'. (*Labour Manifesto*, 1964).	Up 14 per cent., in England, 9 per cent., in Scotland. Labour's new Rating Bill will increase the burden of most ratepayers, in some cases by 5d. in £.
Social Security ' One of our first jobs will be to introduce a new ' income guarantee ' '.	Postponed till at least 1967. *George Brown's* National plan says that ' An incomes guarantee would not contribute to faster economic growth '.

DON'T BE FOOLED AGAIN

Conservatives will . . . .

REDUCE THE BURDEN OF TAXATION —

When in power, income tax was cut five times and purchase tax slashed.

STABILISE THE COST OF LIVING —

Between 1958 and 1964, the cost of living in Britain rose less than in almost any European country.

MORE HOMES FOR OWNER OCCUPATION AND FOR RENT AND A GOVERNMENT ASSISTED SLUM-CLEARANCE PROGRAMME.

Conservatives built more than 4 million new homes and demolished 600,000 slums.

A REGULAR REVIEW OF ALL PENSIONS TO SEE THAT THEY MAINTAIN THEIR PURCHASING POWER. SPECIAL HELP FOR THOSE IN SPECIAL NEED ? LIKE THE OLD PEOPLE WHO EVEN NOW HAVE NO BASIC PENSION.

When in power, Conservatives raised the pension five times and the real value of the pension went up by a half.

And remember, Conservatives keep their promises

so, VOTE FOR

EDWARD TAYLOR

setting up of devolved Parliaments in Scotland and Wales, the issues are considered to be so significant that the House of Commons as a whole will do the Committee's job. However most Bills go to the Committees and the membership of the Committees reflects almost exactly the political balance in the House of Commons.

But how are the Committees really selected? In theory, the Committee of Selection carries out this task and is regarded as being independent. On the other hand, they usually take advice from the Party Whips. However, most of those who spoke on the second reading debate can expect to serve on the committee unless they indicate that they have no interest. Members of the Committee, after appointment, can proceed to put down amendments, which they hope the Committee will consider and approve. In fairness, most of the amendments are tabled by the official Opposition spokesmen, while Government Ministers themselves put down amendments which might stem from reviews within the department, or as a result of representations made to Ministers after the publication of the legislation.

The Committee meets under the control and supervision of an independent chairman – who is an MP on the chairman's panel – and they start off the proceedings by calling for a debate on the first proposed change at the beginning of the legislation. It might be a simple proposal like clause 1, page 1, line 1 – take out the word "may" and insert the word "shall". There would be a debate and a vote on whether the legislation should be so altered. Then we would move on to changes proposed in the next part of the Bill.

An Opposition which is opposed to the legislation, may choose to flood the Order Paper with amendments designed simply to delay its passage. Such delaying tactics are real because a Bill has to complete all its stages, including the proceedings of the House of Lords, in one session, which usually begins in October and ends in July. If, because of the delaying tactics, the proceedings get bogged down, some all night sittings are the norm, and if this does not help progress, the Government can propose a "Guillotine" Motion, restricting the time available for the Committee. The result is that if the Guillotine is approved by Parliament, then a huge number of amendments might not be discussed at all. What usually happened then was that the Government would complain that the opponents of the legislation had been irresponsible and had wasted Parliament's time, while the Opposition would argue that the Government was trampling on the toes of freedom and liberty.

In fairness, this traditional aspect of Parliamentary procedures has virtually died since Mr Blair introduced motions at the same time as second reading determining a programme of debate with perhaps three weeks for the Committee and a week for the continuing Commons procedures. The new time limiting proposal has certainly made life easier for the Government and has deprived the Opposition of one of its greatest weapons. The other result has been to place greater significance on the House of Lords procedures because opponents of legislation now find that the Lords, which is less under the control of government, can sometimes provide the kind of controlled opposition which the Commons used to.

In fairness, whether operating under a timetable or not, the Committee procedures of legislation are a wonderful educative process for MPs. Often they can learn from listening to the speeches and from

Ministerial replies, a great deal about a subject, which they may not have known much about beforehand. Attendance at all the debates in Committee, particularly for Government back-benchers, is essential, because a minimum attendance is required if progress is going to be made.

All amendments must be related to what is called the short title of the Bill. Any other amendments are ruled out of order. For example, if there is a Bill published, called The Council House Bill, and is described in the short title as a Bill to enable council tenants to buy their own homes, it would be perfectly possible to propose an amendment urging that the Bill should not apply to homes built specially for pensioners, but on the other hand, an amendment proposing that more money should be spent on council housing, would be declared out of order and could not be debated.

Once the Committee proceedings have been completed, the Bill then goes through to the next stage, called the Report stage. This is the procedure which allows the Committee to report back to the Commons, listing the various changes which they had made to it and providing, in a debate of the whole House, for the proposed changes to be reviewed and for other changes, which had not been considered in Committee, to be looked at.

Once the Report Stage has been completed, and often on the same evening, there is the Third Reading of the Bill in which MPs determine whether the Bill is still a good Bill after all the changes that have been made.

If the majority vote "Aye" the Bill then goes to the House of Lords where the same procedure is gone through. The House of Lords then reports to the Commons whether they have agreed with the

Bill or not and if there are any further changes to the measure which they would suggest. Sometimes these amendments are controversial and the proposals will go back and forward from the Lords to the Commons in a kind of ping-pong situation. In fairness, if the Lords insist that they do not like the legislation, the Government can apply for a special facility to overturn the Lords' opinions. Such a procedure under the Parliament Act can involve a delay for a year in the legislation and Governments always try to avoid such a level of disagreement and seek a form of compromise.

There are some other aspects of the Parliamentary day which deserve a mention.

First, there is the issue of lunch. In the first 35 years I enjoyed at the House, lunch was something special and interesting. We had at least an hour and a half for a start between the Committees and the beginning of proceedings at 2.30pm and for the younger members the special privilege was to go and sit at a table with the older and more experienced MPs and benefit from their wisdom and specialist knowledge. In the old days almost everyone seemed to go to the Dining-Room for lunch, but things changed. For a start, lunch, except on a Monday, is now when the House is sitting and you feel rather guilty looking up at the notice board and observing who is speaking and what the subject is.

Eating, however, is still rather special. You can go, either to the Members Dining-Room, where strict segregation is applied, or else you can go to the Easy Eats help yourself cafeteria where we do not have menus, waitresses or tablecloths. You can sit wherever you want, even with MPs from the Opposition parties and with friends from the constituency or elsewhere.

But it is different in the Dining-Room.

Up there on the left-hand side, there are many tables where only Conservative MPs can sit. On the right-hand side, there are tables where only Labour MPs may sit. We then have a large table in the middle, reserved for the Liberal Democrats and I can well remember the feeling of optimism amongst the Lib Dems after the last election when an extra leaf had to be added to the table to mark their election successes. Like everything else in Parliament, all goes well until something goes wrong. In this case the wrong thing was the arrival in the House of Gwynfor Evans, a delightful Welsh Nationalist. When he came into the Dining-Room, it was explained to him that there was nowhere for him to sit and that he would have to go to the other place. Being a perfect gentleman, as he was, he never complained. However, we then had the arrival of Winnie Ewing, a strong and determined Scottish Nationalist, and she was very angry.

There was a special meeting of the catering committee. They decided that they did not want to establish a Nationalist table because it was thought that this might just encourage more of them to come to the Commons. So they decided to establish what was known as the Minority Parties table and so Winnie and Gwynfor were able to eat with dignity.

However, solutions sometimes never work long term, because after the next election their table had to be shared with Miss Bernadette Devlin, the vivacious and exciting Irish Nationalist and the Reverend Iain Paisley, who also came from Northern Ireland but who was in no sense a nationalist. So we then had to have, what we used to do at school, a staggered lunch hour.

I also found out in one of the early days in the

house that party divisions applied elsewhere. We have a nice tea room where M.P.s enjoy tea and coffee together, and I went to sit down with a few Scottish Labour M.P.s whom I knew well, without realising that segregation of parties applied. As it happens, Harold Wilson suddenly appeared with a cup of coffee and initiated a conversation.

"What's your name?" he said to me, and of course I told him.

"What's your seat?" And I told him that it was Glasgow Cathcart.

"I didn't know that we won that seat," he said. "Well done!"

"No, I'm afraid that you didn't," I explained.

"Well what are you doing sitting with these excellent labour M.P.s."

"They're friends" I explained. Harold, who seemed to find the whole affair exciting, said that it would be a good idea for me to keep having my coffee on the Labour table as it might persuade me to join the party. If you'd like to cross over, he said, you can explain that Harold Wilson has approved you completely.

It was only a fun piece, but I have to say that I spoke a great deal to Harold Wilson over the years and unlike the Press who took a very negative view of him, I always regarded Harold as one of the really pleasant and straight politicians. There are certainly plenty of rascals around but I didn't place him in this category

Another factor in the Parliamentary day is where one sits. The House of Commons spends its first five minutes each day on saying a prayer. It is the same prayer each day and so does not create the same spiritual excitement, but the special factor about Parliamentary prayers is that MPs have the opportunity of placing a prayer card with their name on it on one particular seat and if the member then attends prayers he can reserve that seat for the day. This is particularly helpful during major debates where there are too many members for the available seats. There has also been some criticism, that since we started televising Prime Minister's question time, there has been a huge increase in the demand for prayer places just behind the Prime Minister, so that back benchers can be observed by their constituents.

MPs sit either on the Government side or the Opposition side (the House of Lords is more flexible and has some benches for independents) and they can choose any seat apart from the front benches which are reserved traditionally for the Cabinet and the Shadow Cabinet. However, although MPs have this wide freedom, they usually sit around the same area because this makes it easier for the Speaker to remember their names. Although MPs may only refer to each other by their constituencies (The Hon Member for Cudlip, the Rt Hon Member for St.Georges or the Hon and Gallant Member for Hogshide), the Speaker has to call them by name if he chooses them to speak.

However, there are certain conventions in seating. There is a bench on the Opposition side which is normally reserved for Ulster Members. Again there are two benches or sometimes three reserved for the Liberals.

After prayers, we have question time when MPs can ask the Ministers questions. It is normally the most exciting part of the day. Each Minister is normally on duty once a fortnight and MPs have to table their questions two weeks beforehand. Obviously lots of MPs want to ask questions and so there is a ballot each day when about 20 are successful and these are published in order. You might be a lucky MP and know almost two weeks beforehand if you are going to be called. However, each question is a kind of mini debate with about three or four questions being asked on the subject of the questions. Whenever a question is being asked about 12 to 20 MPs will jump up and look appealingly and lovingly at the Speaker. He will call first the person with the question, which might be a very general one, like "What measures have been taken to improve rail services over the past five years?" After the Minister replies, the MP whose question it is can ask a supplementary question, then three or four of those jumping up will be called to ask their questions. It's a bit of a nightmare for Ministers, because they have no idea which MPs are going to be called on and they will have no information on some of the particular points that are raised.

While each Minister answers questions once a fortnight, the exception is the Prime Minister who answers questions for half an hour each Wednesday. In fairness, before Mr Blair changed things, the PM used to reply to questions twice a week for 15 minutes. Prime Ministers Question time is normally the most noisy part of the Commons proceedings and very few real questions are asked. It tends to be a gladiatorial contest between the Leader of the Opposition and the Prime Minister in which they both try to score points against each other about the issues of the day. Back-benchers also use the brief period as a vehicle for drawing the Prime Minister's attention to issues they feel strongly about and to local problems or achievements in the constituencies. In this connection the Prime Minister always has a "support squad" who will ask helpful and supportive questions like: "Has the

Prime Minister read the report of the CBI which forecasts higher output and more jobs, and is this not a clear sign of the success of government policies?" Likewise the Opposition usually has an "awkward squad" who will ask questions like: "Has the Prime Minister seen the report of the working party which states that housing conditions in the inner cities are worse than in Victorian times, and is this not a clear sign of the total failure of the Government to solve the housing crisis and its callous disregard for the problems of working people?"

Now that the Prime Minister's Question Time is broadcast, it is becoming more like a football match with each side cheering its team and applauding goals scored.

After Questions, we usually have either a government statement on policy or a Private Notice Question. If there has been some emergency, like an explosion in a factory, or a collapse of the currency, a Member may seek the Speaker's permission to ask an emergency question. Likewise, if a Government Minister wishes to announce an important new government policy initiative, or the publication of a White Paper on policy, he will make a statement in the House and subject himself to questions from back-benchers.

Following these items, the House usually embarks on the major debate of the day. In each week there are normally three days allocated to the Government, one day, or part of it to one of the Opposition Parties, and there is one day for Private Members (almost always a Friday).

If it is a debate on a Government Bill or motion, the Minister will introduce the subject in a half hour speech. The Opposition spokesman will then give his reply. Then the back-benchers debate begins and it goes on until the Speaker – about 40 minutes before the vote, calls on the front bench spokesman to sum up their case.

In a normal day, about 20 to 30 MPs will try to speak and about 10 will be called. The Speaker is always wholly fair in his selection, but preference is normally given to Privy Councillors (usually ex Ministers) and to minority parties or groups. There is no more depressing activity, than sitting through an entire debate but not being called on to speak.

At the end of the debate, which is usually now 10pm on a Monday or 7pm on other days, we have the vote. We do not put up our hands, or press electronic buttons. The MPs have to walk through one of two long corridors to vote either Aye or No. While it is a time consuming exercise, like most of our apparently silly customs, it has a lot of merit.

For a start, the procedure means that we know exactly who votes, which way, and who was not there to vote. The detailed lists are published in Hansard, and no MP can say he voted on the spur of the moment. Finally, everyone has to go through the lobbies, including the Prime Minister and his Cabinet and this gives MPs a rather unique opportunity to press issues and make representations. One example which certainly comes to mind, is when Mrs Thatcher was Prime Minister. The Southend Council had decided, after lengthy consideration, to go ahead with a plan to improve and develop our very long pier which is well over a mile long. Sadly, a few days after the decision, the Government announced a freeze on capital spending. If I had written to a Minister to ask for a meeting, it could have taken weeks to arrange, but I took the opportunity during a vote to speak to the Prime Minister. She promised to look at the matter urgently and happily the pier restoration plan went ahead.

After the major vote, the Commons moves on to less weighty matters. We used to have a lot of 90 minute debates on Regulations, which are a kind of mini legislation stemming from powers in the law, but these now rarely occur and are instead dealt with by motions. However, what we still have after the Commons day is what is referred to as the adjournment debate. The half hour is allocated to one MP who has 30 minutes at his disposal and he can select the issues of his choice. It may be a big international issue like famine relief. Or it may be a minor one like the refusal of the Government to approve a zebra crossing in a borough. The MP speaks to a House which is usually empty, apart from the official Government Minister responsible and usually a Whip.

The Minister then replies. The day is then over. The Sergeant at Arms calls the traditional cry of "Who Goes Home?" It is said that this tradition stems from the olden times when London streets were unsafe, when MPs were unpopular and when the MPs going home used to gather round a lantern and marched along to their homes protected by a little platoon of soldiers.

Hours in Parliament, although a lot easier since the Blair reforms, are still quite long and exhausting, because there are often lots of meetings on policy and on issues of significance after the House rises. On the other hand, there are long recesses. Again it is an old tradition. MPs used to have to travel for days to reach Parliament from their homes or constituencies, and naturally preferred to get the business over in as few days as possible, and then to travel back to home and constituency. Modern travel has placed most MPs within a few hours from their constituencies, but the old customs prevail, and as always there is a strong and deep-rooted opposition to changing them. Perhaps the most aggressive in opposing change is the Government, whose Ministers welcome breaks from questions and speeches from MPs!

12

The EEC dimension

Britain's decision to join the EEC was historic and controversial and I was very much involved in the controversy at the time. The arguments about whether it was in Britain's interest to become a full member of the Common Market will probably go on for decades. There have to be arguments in the absence of proof because, of course, there is no way in which we can establish what Britain's position would have been if we had remained outside the Community.

However, there is certainly no controversy at all about the basic fact that membership has eroded and restricted the powers of national decision making by each of the Parliaments of the member states, and in consequence, of the rights of individual Members of Parliament.

Before membership, there was, in theory, no limitation on the powers of Parliament. Although certain laws and decisions were not made because they were not prudent or might unnecessarily upset other countries, Parliament was basically at liberty to do what it liked. There was no written constitution and no curbs on the powers of Parliament, to legislate, or on MPs to seek to promote changes in government policy.

Every decision made by Britain, and every law passed, had to be approved by Parliament and was subject to scrutiny in detail, but membership of the EEC has changed this.

For a start, we have, in effect, a written constitution with the Treaty of Rome and the other Treaties passed in the interim. No law, regulation or decision can be made which conflicts with the Treaty. Nor can we pass laws which conflict with decisions made by the Council of Ministers or Regulations approved by the EEC. The only way of changing these would be to get every member state of the EEC to agree to a change.

Now, of course, there are many examples which could be quoted, but I will mention three representative ones which came on to my desk in January 1986.

First, I had a post card from a constituent urging me to press in Parliament for the outlawing of the LD 50 test. This is a test used for new drugs and preparations under which quantities of the drug or preparation are given to a controlled group of animals – perhaps rats or monkeys – until 50 percent of the animals die. A note is then taken of the amount of the drug which is given to the animals before half of them die from the effects. Now of course there are arguments both ways on this issue. On the one hand, some argue that it is quite intolerable to inflict such suffering on innocent animals. Others argue that without such a test, we might find that new drugs could kill off many innocent human beings.

The plain fact is that no matter what I or other MPs think, we cannot change the LD 50 test, which is an EEC law or regulation. In short, Parliament has lost its sovereignty.

Secondly, I had a plea from the Essex Bee-keepers Association complaining bitterly about the huge taxpayers subsidies devoted to subsidising the export of very cheap sugar to the Soviet Union while the Essex Bee-keepers have to pay the very high EEC price for their sugar. The high cost of sugar, they advise me, will make bee-keeping wholly uneconomical in Britain.

Sadly there is not one thing I can do about it. Even if every MP in the Commons voted to deplore the sugar subsidies, it would have no effect. The export levies which give cheap sugar to Russia and the high import levies which force up the UK price are an integral part of the Common Market's Agricultural policy. Again, it could only be changed if every member state agreed to do so.

Thirdly, I had a plea from a local hotel operator. She argues that it is ridiculous that the exemption level of VAT is as low as £19,000 turnover. She has to pay a lot of VAT on the sums she charges her boarders, but she cannot claim back much because VAT is not payable on most of the items she buys, like food.

A Treasury Minister has sent me a reply to this enquiry, indicating that the Government would look with favour on a higher VAT exemption level, but sadly they could not do so unless EEC rules were changed.

These are only three small examples of the restrictions on our freedom. Now of course, there are many who would argue that this is a step forward to European Government and a retreat from narrow nationalism. They would argue that common laws and common standards are good for Europe and thereby good for Britain.

However, the fact of the loss of sovereignty for the British Parliament remains.

Apart from these restrictions on Parliamentary freedom of action, we also have a major change in the manner in which decisions are made. Decisions in the EEC are made, broadly, at meetings of the Council of Ministers. A Minister representing each nation sits round a table and they argue back and forward until they arrive at a compromise. It may be a meeting of the Industry Council, at which a new plan for steel regulation is made, or a meeting of the Agriculture Council, where decisions on farm support are made, or a meeting of the Trade Council where decisions are made on import quotas from Japan. Or it could be a meeting of the Council of Environment Ministers agreeing on new standards for the emission of smoke from chimneys. Sometimes there is horse-trading, with one nation agreeing to support another in the Agriculture Council in exchange for similar support the other way in the Finance Council.

The fact is, that the laws are made and the new regulations sorted out in detail at meetings of Ministers. The House of Commons and its MPs are utterly irrelevant.

So when the eventual regulation is reported back, MPs have a fait accompli. They may have detailed proposals of how the steel regime should be changed, or the smoke regulations improved, but all the discussion has taken place. Brussels has done the First Reading, the Committee Stage, the Third Reading and the Lords Amendment in one fell swoop.

Even the power to reject the proposals is suspect. It has not happened up till now with Government forcing through their agreed Brussels compromises. However, even if Parliament did reject one of the packages, it is probable that Britain could be taken to the European Court for non-implementation of the agreed formula.

I think that MPs are among the few who realise, because of their participation in law making, the full scale of the loss of sovereignty and of their inability even to influence decisions on vital issues. Step by step, the British Parliament is becoming a kind of grand county council with the major policies being decided in Brussels. It may be for good of ill, but it is one of the greatest constitutional changes ever to hit democracy.

13

The work in constituencies

Anyone thinking of becoming an MP should appreciate that a very major part of the job is well away from the glamour of Parliament and can involve the most humdrum and tedious duties, but constituency work is a vital vehicle for keeping an MP's feet on the ground and for learning from voters about their fears, their worries and their aspirations.

The scale of the work depends directly on whether the MP chooses to live in his constituency and to be generally available to constituents, when Parliament is not sitting, or stay in London and to make visits to the constituency from time to time. It is a major decision to make, because the workload is infinitely greater for those MPs who live "in the parish". Conversely, an MP who lives in another place can get out of touch with what is happening locally and also tends to gauge constituency opinion from the letters he receives from the small minority who take the trouble to write. Put more crudely, I find as a "live in" MP, that I learn much more about what people are thinking from what my wife hears from friends when doing her shopping or calling to collect children from school than from what I learn from meeting "representative" groups or committees which are rarely really representative of those they claim to speak for. You learn more from a chat with teachers in a school staff room during a break than you do from meeting the local committee of the National Union of Teachers.

Much of the burden of the "live in" MP falls on the wife and family who have to attend to the telephone calls which flood in – usually when the meal is on the table or the child is being bathed. The wife of a "live in" MP tends to get invited to visit or speak at local bodies and functions. The availability is the key. Quite recently we had a phone call at home from a person in a nearby constituency who had a most urgent problem because her electricity was about to be cut off and she was anxious that enquiries should be made about the possibility of her paying off the bill by instalments. It was 10pm on a Sunday night. I had to explain that as she lived in another constituency, I was precluded under Commons rules from taking up the case, but I suggested that she might wish to ring up her own MP and offered to give her the London phone number. "Do you not think he would mind me phoning him at his home?" was the response. "But you are phoning me at my home," I pointed out. But somehow it was different. A local MP is regarded as being available in a way in which the non-resident MP is not – and somehow people don't worry about phoning the MP if their child is at the same school as the MP's or if there is some other relationship with the enquirer.

There has certainly been a significant change in constituency attitudes since I first went to Parliament. Quite a few selection committees insist that any candidate selected should make his main home in the constituency, while in former days, an MP living locally was rather an oddity.

What work does an MP have to do in his constituency? For a start, he must be available for interview by constituents on a regular basis. I have always had a weekly surgery for constituents on a Saturday morning. On an average Saturday in Glasgow we tended to have about 40 callers, while in Southend, it is about 25. Looking into all the problems does take a lot of time, because for a start, there are usually at least two letters to send – one to the constituent to say what is being done about his problem and the other, perhaps more than one, to the department, board, landlord or local council who can provide the information or decision required. It is very rare for cases to be resolved simply by discussion. Even if someone calls to ask for your views on some current Parliamentary issue, they normally prefer to receive the assurance in writing, but most callers have personal problems with some kind of official body or department.

Of course there are the minority with mental or psychological problems. I well remember one of my regular callers in Glasgow who went through agonies because the "secret service" had got control of his wavelength and forced him to go places and do things against his will. More recently I have had a haunted soul calling regularly because Arthur Scargill and three Arabs came down her chimney every night for the specific purpose of pulling her hair – although they were clearly unsuccessful as could be seen from her very full head of dishevelled hair.

Of course there are the impossible cases to resolve. People who complain about the noise made by neighbours or their dogs. People who insist that they have been deprived of some tax benefit years ago and refuse to accept even the clearest and most detailed explanation given by the Chancellor of the Exchequer himself in a letter signed by himself. Then there are the tragic cases of small businesses facing ruin because of a multitude of unpaid bills and an absence of revenue to cover them – when the proprietors come along to the MP as their "last hope", in the expectation that some Government Board or

Department is suddenly going to cascade taxpayers cash down a chute to resolve the problem.

However, in most cases, it is possible to make some progress. Government Departments, local organisations, state boards. Local Councils and even local landlords do usually try to make some concession, wherever possible, in response to an MP's letter.

For the very conscientious MP, however, there is a real danger that in being a good social worker, he will spend all his available constituency time seeing the minority of his constituents with problems and dictating letters about these problems instead of having time to keep in touch with the majority who never trouble MPs with any problems.

There's more to constituency work than just holding on to the seat. My friends and I also thought there was a crusade to guide the party and to keep in touch with the people.

We had quite a number of political meetings in Cathcart and we always seemed to attract very large audiences in the Couper Institute. This large public hall was always significant to me because it was there, when I was six years of age, that I signed the pledge to renounce alcohol, and I got a lovely pound note for doing it. Teetotalism was a major community issue in Glasgow, where we were aware of the evils of drinking. I've always stuck to the pledge and never consumed even a glass of wine; probably one of the main factors in this was not just the pledge or the pound, but the fact that one of my first bosses was someone with a serious drink problem, who frequently told me that he had given it up but who sadly died at quite an early age. Knowing his skills and abilities and the nightmares which alcohol created for him, teetotalism seemed sensible and prudent.

What was special about our public meetings? Of course every constituency endeavoured to invite leading party members to their annual meeting, annual dinners and other gatherings of party members and supporters. And invariably the speakers would tell the faithful that they had a splendid leader, a splendid party, a splendid M.P., and that everything, including the weather, would get much worse if the opposition parties were to do well. But being more of a crusading movement, we endeavoured to hold meetings which would be open to everyone, and at which interesting political ideas would be advanced. Apart from the speech and the questions, the only other activity was an appeal for finance to pay the costs of such meetings and we had a big army of collectors. The particular joy for me was that to save funds the speakers used to spend the night at my home and usually had a meal there as well. Shortly after I became the M.P. I purchased for my mother and myself a little terrace house in Craig Road and this is where the exciting politicians came to stay with us.

One of our successful events was a visit by Enoch Powell. He cheered my mother up enormously by telling her that the lunch she made for us was "well above the standards of the House of Commons" However, after the lunch was over Enoch explained that as we had a couple of hours to spare he would much enjoy having the opportunity of seeing some of the historic aspects of Cathcart. "What is there to see and where should we go?" he said with some passion. I had been hoping to take him to Castlemilk, our massive housing estate, but in an endeavour to satisfy his request, I told him that we had a large and rather old cemetery not far from our home, which had a big wall round it, and where people had been buried for a very long time. He seemed to find this fascinating, and so we walked up to the Old Cathcart Cemetery and walked through the very imposing iron gates. He kept on looking at the stones, some of which were obviously large and exciting for architectural historians. Eventually I persuaded him that time was going on and that he would have to come back to our home if he wanted to go over his speech before the public meeting. However, as we walked back I saw to my horror that the Iron Gates had been closed and locked, a practice which was a response to a minority of hooligans who enjoyed destroying things. Is there another door he asked? I shook my head and started wondering what on earth we would say at the public meeting,

But Enoch was a tough guy. He stood on top of one of the stones, then climbed up on top of the wall. I followed him. After we had both clambered over the wall and started our walk back home, Enoch smiled and said to me "What a massive opportunity these photographers have lost. If they could have taken my picture when climbing over the wall, and published it on their front page, they could have had a wonderful headline "Enoch climbs Out of the Dead'

We had a great meeting that night: his subject was public expenditure. What particularly seemed to please the audience was that he had obviously prepared the talk thoroughly, and he also took the opportunity to mention a sizeable number of examples of spending in Scotland.

We also had a delightful visit from Ted Heath shortly after he became leader of the Party. It was all a bit strange because we didn't invite him at all. What happened was that our central office phoned me to say that they had phoned my Conservative Office to say that he was coming to Scotland, that he had some free time on a Sunday and was there anything helpful he could do for us. The Party office kindly told the head office to speak to me. In a display of rather silly pomposity, I pointed out that we didn't do political things in Cathcart on a Sunday and that if he wanted to visit us he should come with me to the Cathcart Parish church. I thought that this would produce a negative result, but strange to say it seemed that Ted was delighted and he came along in his car to meet us outside the church. I ensured that we had quite a few of our supporters there and the whole episode was a great success. There was a splendid sermon, the church people seemed delighted that we had not put on any display like hand shaking or official welcomes, and there were no press handouts.

The episode got me off to a good relationship with Ted Heath and although we seemed to disagree politically on almost everything, we were always the best of friends and remained so even after I resigned from his government when he decided to join the European Union.

We didn't just invite politicians to speak at our meetings - we sometimes invited non politicians who had interesting views and who were regarded as interesting by the general public. One such visitor was Patrick Moore, who knew all about the skies and their contents. He attracted a large audience and fascinated them by a whole series of stories about French and German characters in history and more recent times.

An MP who wishes to keep the confidence of his electors must make a point of attending meetings of constituents of all sorts, rotary clubs, lunch clubs, local factories, local schools, pensioners groups, Chamber of Commerce, sporting clubs, council departments and local shopkeepers. Only in this way can he keep abreast of their views and attitudes which he must bear very much in mind in his Parliamentary work. Then there are the public services like the electricity boards, British Rail and so on. Personal contact can be particularly helpful if a constituency problem arises in which the assistance of the Board is required.

Then there is the political side too. The MP must remember that he is selected for his job, not just by the voters but also by his local constituency party, without whose help and support he would not even be a candidate. MPs who neglect their local parties can often find to their horror that the power points in the local constituency party have been taken over by hostile elements – a problem more relevant at the present time to the Labour Party, but just as important is a less dramatic and ideological way within the Conservative Party. The MP must not forget that he owes a special debt to the many voluntary workers who are prepared to knock on doors and deliver pamphlets plus raising funds to ensure the eventual re-election victory if all goes well.

Last of all, there is the obligation to communicate. Voters and Party officials nowadays expect their MPs to have a reasonably high profile. The great mystery of Parliament has evaporated, and if local people do not read in local papers or see or listen to the radio to their local MPs, they gain the impression that he is not working as hard as he should. This is particularly important in the 1960s when there is the emergence of a third force in British politics, virtually wiping out the previous rather comfortable arrangement whereby there were around 150 Tory and about 140 Labour cast iron "safe" seats in good times and bad. In these times of political change, there are very few seats which can now be regarded as wholly safe, and no MP can afford to relax. Quite apart from the electoral consideration, an MP has a duty to keep people informed about what he is trying to do for them in Parliament. It is like every other job. If you cannot continue to convince your employers that you are doing a reasonable job in exchange for your salary, the prospect of redundancy or dismissal is always there.

A pair of right Teds!

14

On becoming a Minister

There is something very exciting about first becoming a Minister in a Government. For a start, it is an opportunity to move into the circles of decision-making which a back-bench MP is necessarily excluded from. It is also a form of promotion and an indication that at least in the eyes of the Prime Minister, you have been doing well as a back-bencher and have special qualities to contribute. The promotion gives just the hint of even greater things to come. A successful Junior Minister is obviously on the short list for further promotion when the vacancies arise in the course of time or reshuffles take place. It is rather like being made a foreman in a factory or a prefect at school.

And so it was for me, when in 1970, Ted Heath phoned me and asked if I would be one of his Under Secretaries of State for Scotland, with special responsibility for education and health.

In fairness, my elevation to office was not quite so significant as South of the Border, because there were four Scottish jobs which had to be filled by a small band of Scottish Conservative MPs, which meant that all Scottish Tories who were not alcoholics, womanisers or illiterates had a reasonable prospect of securing office at some stage of their Parliamentary careers.

However, on the other hand, the Scottish jobs were in some ways of greater interest than National Government posts because with all functions, except Treasury, Trade and Foreign Affairs, being effectively devolved to the Scottish Office, Ministers North of the Border had a much wider remit than their colleagues in the South.

10 DOWNING STREET

10 Feb.

Dear Teddy,

Thank you for your
kind invitation to your
Ladies Lunch in June/
July.

For obvious reasons
I NEVER make polit-
ical speeches beyond a
3 minute message
from the P.M.' For

10 Feb [1982]

Dear Teddy,

Thank you for your kind invitation to your Ladies Lunch in June/July.
For obvious reasons I NEVER make political speeches beyond a 3 minute "Message from the P.M.". Far less would I, or could I follow Cecil or other Cabinet "stars" to whom your Ladies are accustomed. Thus I am always a silent, or almost silent, a Guest which means you have to find another speaker in an addition to your brilliant self. If you think I can do any good by "meeting and greeting" as many of your Ladies as I can then I shall happily find a day in June to do so.
Teddy, I will not be in the least offended if you say "no deal" 'cos I know silent Guests are no draw on these occasions.

> Regards, as ever,
> Denis

Letter from Denis Thatcher, 1982

Ted Heath paying a visit to Glasgow. I was one of his junior ministers when I had to resign over the Treaty of Rome in 1971

The first thing that happens after your appointment is that someone comes on to the phone to explain that he is your private secretary and suggests that you should, as soon as possible, visit the Ministries for which you are now responsible.

These private secretaries are carefully chosen from the younger ranks of the civil service high flyers and they have a vitally important task to perform. For a start, they must explain all the procedural ropes to the new Minister and they have to report promptly and clearly to Departmental heads any thoughts expressed by Ministers and any initiatives which they are taking with other Government colleagues. They also have to record every meeting which is held, and even every conversation which their Minister has on the telephone – and circulate the details to those concerned in the issues discussed, so that good communications are maintained.

This was all the more important in the Scottish Office because Ministers spent most of their time in London in the Scottish Office in Whitehall, while almost all the civil servants who were implementing the agreed policies worked in St Andrew's House, in Edinburgh.

The private secretary has also a key role in the first few day in explaining all the "does and don'ts", of being a Minister. The first rule is, that from the time of the appointment, the Minister must not express views on any matters outside the boundaries of his responsibility. For example, if a Scottish Minister feels strongly that taxes on beer are too high, that the trade balance with Japan calls for action, or that the latest miners' pay claim should be rejected, he must keep his views to himself, because the responsibility for commenting on these issues rests with other Government colleagues. Also, even within his own field of responsibility, he is advised, in the strongest terms, not to say anything to anyone without taking "advice" from officials, because a Minister's statements would have to be discussed with other Scottish Office colleagues in case they might have revenue consequences or conflict with previous agreed policies. All letters sent out from the office had to be cleared with officials, and even in writing constituency letters, one had to exercise restraint and caution. As a back-bencher, if a constituent wrote to me about South Africa, I would have normally indicated that I was opposed to the imposing of economic sanctions, but once a Minister, one would have to check up with care on the policy of the Government.

In short, the freedom which back-benchers have to let off steam and to express their personal views disappears when they become Ministers.

The next restriction relates to private conversations. Ministers constantly see a mass of papers, some of which are marked "confidential", and even "secret", with "restricted" being the lowest security classification. A Minister must never reveal or even hint at issues raised in these papers in his private conversations with colleagues. A "leak" of policy being considered by Ministers could have the most embarrassing consequences for the Government. This is, in some ways, the most difficult part. If a colleague and friend mentions that there is an urgent unemployment problem in his area, a Minister cannot reveal to him any details of private discussions which may be proceeding in St Andrew's House designed to attract a new American firm to the area.

Every statement of policy or any announcement must be made in a formal and official way.

Ministers are also warned of security dangers, and I will never forget the conversation I had with a rather seedy and weak looking character who claimed to be on the "security side", who was given the task of explaining to me, in graphic detail, the kind of compromising situations which nasty Russians or their agents would endeavour to entice Ministers into, as a means of getting a blackmailing hold on the Ministers and thereby possibly securing access to Government secrets.

But within hours, the real work begins. First the new Minister is given a "position paper" setting out the state of play in the Department's affairs – the Bills which they had in preparation for presenting to the Commons, the problems which they had, and the issues on which they were seeking to get the agreement of Treasury and other colleagues to establish as "policy".

Happily for me, at that time, there were few crises facing my section of the Scottish Office, although it was explained that I would have to take personal responsibility for piloting a Bill through the Commons to give local councils the right to charge fees for tuition at certain schools. This was the consequence of an election promise, although it seemed a bit daft, for the simple reason, that no local council in Scotland had expressed the slightest interest in charging fees in any of their schools.

The other "issue" on the sports side (because I was the Scottish Sports Minister as well as Education, Health and Social Work Minister) was the possibility of a national football stadium being established, with some government support, at the famous Hampden Park, home of the Queens Park Football Club, which was, and still is, the only amateur team in any of the football leagues.

But the position paper did not give the true picture. There was a horrendous workload.

The Parliamentary duties of attendance continued, and in some respects were greater, because the Party Whips expect the "payroll" vote of Ministers and Parliamentary Private Secretaries to be present and to vote on these late night complicated Bills, from which some back-benchers would feel justified in absenting themselves. The constituency work continued as before, with the flood of letters and enquiries, and on top of this there was the Ministerial load, the Scottish part of it concentrated on Fridays and during recesses.

In London, during the week, there was the flood of correspondence and submissions to deal with. Instead of my writing to Ministers, I had to reply to the letters about constituency problems or issues. Others would just send on their constituent's letters direct with remarks written on the top like – "Isn't this unfair?" or "Do you think that my constituent has a point?" or even the less dramatic, "Reply, please!" Ministers usually read all the letters so that they can be prepared if the MP speaks to them about the correspondence in the lobbies. Nothing destroys the credibility or acceptance of a Minister more than if an MP has tortured himself over the wording of a letter to a Minister and then finds a few days later that the Minister cannot even recall seeing the correspondence. Of course, the replies are drafted by civil servants, although the Minister can query the drafts of replies and give some general advice like an instruction that he wishes his replies in general, to be courteous and sympathetic, even if the enquiry is a daft one. He may also give guidance as to the manner in which insulting or harsh political letters from Opposition members should be replied to. Through time, the civil servants get a general picture of what kind of replies the Minister likes. Of course, in theory, the Minister can demand changes to these letters and seek discussions with his officials, but such discussions invariably take up more time, and at the end of the day, the Minister is presented with the point that the change he wishes might be against "agreed government policy" or could involve extra public expenditure not allowed for. When Ministers find that the challenging of draft letters involves them in meetings with civil servants, memos to other Ministers and even discussions with Ministerial colleagues, he finds that there is a positive disincentive to question official advice.

Then there are the official submissions from civil servants about new policy initiatives or decisions for which they seek general Ministerial approval. I have always found that the civil servants are of a high standard and play the game in always securing Ministerial approval for what they do, but again, the system limits the Minister's freedom to make his own choice.

A submission might be about five sheets of careful wording putting a series of options, but the arguments invariably seemed to go in the direction of one option. The submission might, for example, be about health centres. The submission might, for example, under this general heading, explain that because the Treasury had decided to cut down on health service spending in Scotland, action would need to be taken to curb existing programmes. The paper would point out that with the pattern of agreed contracts, the scope for action would be limited. They might specify that three things could be done to save the £3,000,000 demanded by the Treasury. First, there could be a decision to close down a facility providing medical treatment for sick children suffering from leukaemia. Second, it could be decided to make a charge for patients travelling to hospital in ambulances. Or third, there could be a decision to delay the building of two health centres in Dundee and Aberdeen. The submission would go on to say that there were already three health centres in both cities and that the worst that could happen, in consequence of the cancelling of the two health centres, was that residents in these cities would be required to make a journey of an additional five minutes. It would also point out that the health centre programme had already been expanded furiously because of increases in available spending over the previous three years and that if challenged, Ministers could point out that the Government's health centre programme was twice as large as that in the previous government of the other party.

The submission would end with the explanation that the decision was entirely one for the Ministers and that the Department would be glad to receive their instructions!

So there we see the power of Ministers. To decide whether to bash sick children suffering from leukaemia, to make disabled people and accident victims pay for their ambulances, or to cancel two large health centres which would involve minimum inconvenience. The submission would be sent round to all the Scottish Office Ministers and they would have to write their comments.

One of the Ministers might represent Aberdeen and might write on his submission "Why Aberdeen?" Could we not cancel one on the West Coast instead of two in the East?" This would prompt a note from the Department – again copied to all Ministers – explaining that sadly the centres in the West had already been contracted for and that cancellation would involve extra spending in compensation and might also involve people in the West having to travel forty miles to their nearest ones. However, the Department would bear in mind the injustice done to Aberdeen when considering future programmes.

Another may write – "Was the expansion of health centres not a priority in our election manifesto, and are there really no other items of expenditure which could be pruned?" Again, a note from the civil servants, explaining that they had sifted through all the possibilities, but that the only options were bashing the sick children or charging patients for their ambulances. However, if Ministers would prefer these alternatives, the Department would, of course, be glad to prepare details of an ambulance charging scheme which, on further inspection, would involve a charge of £22 per ambulance ride to achieve the desired savings.

But a really difficult Minister might put in a note saying that he understood from gossip or from a cutting in a local paper that the Department had plans to build a hospital for the treatment of businessmen suffering from stress and excessive eating. Why could this not be cancelled instead? Again, a note would come back. While it was true, the note would say, that there was such a plan, the Prime Minister herself had spoken at the CBI Conference and made it clear that the Government regarded the business stress and over-eating treatment service for top executives as a key priority because of the impact on our exports, of top business executives being off work as a consequence of over-eating, and that the cancellation of the programme would really require Downing Street approval. However, if the Ministers wished to pursue this, a meeting could be held in

Auchtermuchty the following Tuesday at 8.30am with Professor Plonk of the over-eating special study, so that Ministers could be advised of the position in detail, before seeking a meeting next Tuesday (sadly unavoidable because Professor Plonk was about to depart for a three week conference on over-eating in San Francisco on the Tuesday afternoon) when the Commons was sitting till midnight on the Monday and was facing up to an all night sitting on the Tuesday, would probably deter the Minister from pursuing the issue, and even if the journey was undertaken, the next step would have to be a meeting with the busy Prime Minister to persuade him/her to abandon one of his/her current brain-childs – and this is not the most agreeable task for any Minister.

So, almost inevitably and consistently, the submission would be approved. Ministers had indeed exercised their power!

I do not relate this tale to attack civil servants. The fact is that they tend to know a great deal more about priorities and options than Ministers and they obviously study the issues in detail before making recommendations. However, what it does show, is that if a Minister wants to get something done, he has to prepare his ground carefully, seek, if possible, to persuade civil servants that he has a point, and persuade his fellow Ministers before discussions actually start, and he has to commit himself to pursue the issue and not be deflected.

I can recall one specific issue which I endeavoured to pursue, but eventually, after hours of discussion and piles of memos, I reluctantly settled for an "enquiry", which itself went on for months. My fault had been not persuading the officials that my concept was a good one – and it is understandable that civil servants should not wish to go along with a policy initiative which they would be obliged to carry out long after the Minister had moved away or moved on.

Looking back on my period of about a year as a Junior Minister, I think it is possible that I may have made some marginal impact on the direction of policy through my comments and proposals, but the only specific issue on which I can claim wholly personal credit, was stopping the closure - by a local council - of Corrie Primary School on the Isle of Arran.

Before a local council can actually close a school, they have to secure the agreement of the Scottish Office Minister. As a regular visitor to Corrie, I was well aware that the school was the focal point of community life. It also appeared that the population of "mainlanders" seeking a quiet life and carrying out a multitude of "Craft" small businesses with the aid of Government funds, might actually increase the school rolls.

I therefore put a note "No, I don't agree!" on the submission and waited for the reaction. None came. Perhaps the civil servants had decided there was some point in giving a minor victory to a Minister who appeared to be becoming frustrated. Or perhaps they simply thought that it did not matter to the Scottish Office, as the extra spending of keeping the school open, would fall on the local council.

It still gives me pleasure to go to the Isle of Arran on holiday and to see the school apparently prospering and full (perhaps not very full) with happy children.

But submissions were only part of the work.

There were the meetings in Edinburgh with deputations. If a group of local councillors, often accompanied by the local MP, had a grievance about

Party policy in my area, they could seek a meeting with the Minister. I was always well briefed, before the meeting, with a paper indicating what they would probably say and what I should, in any event, reply. Again I had the opportunity of discussing "my reply" with the civil servants, and one had to be reasonably clued up so that one could speak from memory. Nothing distresses deputations more than to have a Minister reading out a reply which had obviously been written before the deputation's argument was heard.

Sometimes there was scope for flexibility.

The Minister's draft reply might have at the end, the words "If pressed....." and this would indicate a fall back concession which might be made if the argument did not really sound logical in view of the representations made.

For example, there might be a deputation of local councillors arguing that they did not have enough cash to provide their school meals service and for school cleaning because of the inadequate funds supplied by the Government.

The draft reply might point out that the council concerned was getting as much as five other local councils who seemed to be able to pay for their school cleaning and still have some money in the bank at the end of the year. Was there not perhaps a need for a search for economies in other areas?

However, if the deputation then provided a wholly convincing answer, to the effect that the price of potatoes for school meals and the wages which had to be paid to cleaners, were higher in their areas than in the other authorities referred to, the Minister could produce his fall back answer – probably an assurance that he would report the difficulties being experienced by the council to his

Scottish Office colleagues so that provision might be made in the next rate support grant for extra funds for local councils suffering from high potato prices. There would, of course, be no promise, but the Minister would try to do his best.

Generally it would work out, because the civil servants in the education department, would not normally suggest a fall back answer like this, unless they had already cleared with the Scottish Development Department that such a minor change in the rate support grant formula could be made.

Then there were the conferences. The holding of conferences is one of our growing national diseases and in Scotland they tend to be held in remote hotels where the environmental health officer, the social workers, the police, the probation officers, the nurses or the dog wardens employed by public authorities, can come together once a year for a pleasant break and to discuss their problems with those doing comparable jobs elsewhere.

Most of the conferences have a slot in their programme for a Ministerial speech, setting out the Government's appreciation of the wonderful work done by the conference attendees and setting out the Government's future plans to ensure that the service provided by them would develop and prosper.

It is a real ordeal for the Minister, because often he has to read out a long speech prepared by others on a subject which he does not understand. Ministers are well advised to get away from the conference immediately after their speeches with the excuse of urgent Parliamentary or Ministerial business, to avoid being questioned by the experts at the conference about the significance of the speech which he has made. In theory, Ministers should take the trouble to learn what the speeches are all about and to discuss the issues with the officials, but time is always a nightmare and if a Minister has time to read through a speech before he makes it, he is doing well.

A quick flight is advisable. If, for example, a Minister announces to the environmental health officers that the Government is giving the closest of consideration to the reviewing of Clause 24B of the Housing Act of 1967, in so far as it relates to public sewers in inner city areas, which are not covered by the provisions of section 12 of the Public Health Act of 1938, this may be music to the ears of the environmental health officers, but the Minister can be in a spot if challenged after his speech by the President of the organisation on whether this proposed change will also affect drains in public premises covered by Crown Immunity. Probably he will not have a clue, so it is better that the opportunities for the questions should be avoided.

15

Government decision-making

Another part of a Minister's work is to attend meetings of Cabinet Sub-Committees. While the Cabinet is attended by the top Secretaries of State, the more minor issues are discussed at meetings of Junior Ministers, and Scottish Ministers attend more than their share because most policy decisions have a Scottish dimension.

Ministers attending these meetings are again fully briefed by officials and it is emphasised at all times that they are speaking for their Secretaries of State and Departments and should not start offering their own views on issues which might arise. There are many such committees and they are normally presided over by a Senior Cabinet Member who has the task of reporting the conclusions to the Cabinet.

There is always a clear agenda, and before the meeting takes place, there is a meeting of the Officials Committee to discuss most of the issues. A chief official from each of the Ministries represented at the Cabinet Sub-Committee will be present at this meeting and they usually sort out the issues.

Say, for example, there is a meeting on the Home Affairs Sub-Committee, there might be three items on the agenda. First there might be the issue of compensation for flood damage. Second, drug abuse. Thirdly, Police pay.

On the first, my paper might indicate that the Government had allocated £20 million for flood relief and that my task would be to ensure that a higher than proportional sum of the cash should come to Scotland because the rain had been heavier there.

We would all say our piece and I would record, in

graphic detail, from my notes that farmers had been stranded in boats, that schools had been flooded and that old aged pensioners halls had been devastated. I would also recall that the level of rain in Scotland had been twice the national average and that only Cumbria in England had suffered so much.

The Cabinet Minister would beam and look thoughtful, but after we had all made our pleas, he would probably report that the official committee had met the hour before and drafted a scheme which would offer a scheme of compensation of £20 per farmer, £40 per school and £60 per OAP hall, but that in Scotland and Cumbria the figures would be 50 per cent more.

Did this seem acceptable to colleagues?

We would hastily look at our notes to see if there was any reference to percentages, and if, as would probably be the case, my paper asked me to argue for 50 per cent more, I would agree with all the others.

We would then come to drug abuse. The Chairman would report that the Home Secretary in consultation with the Scottish Secretary (a smile to me) had drafted a Bill to make provision for new drug treatment centres. Copies of the proposed Bill had been circulated and would be published next week. Were there any comments?

My notes might say that the nasty Department of Health and Social Security was pressing for the bill to make specific provision for four of the centres to be in England and only one in Scotland, and that I should press for there to be no reference to numbers in the bill because the Department was hoping to argue with the Treasury for two in Scotland.

The Health Junior Minister would embark on his argument saying that it was regrettable that the Bill made no mention of the number of treatment centres in each part of the UK and that he considered that Clause 2 should be amended to provide specifically for four centres in England and one in Scotland.

Then I would jump in to say that it would be wrong to specify numbers as extra funds might become available in the future and we might find that we needed more than five centres in the country as a whole. The Chairman would appear to be deeply pensive and thoughtful as though a mighty and insoluble problem had been placed before him.

Turning to his official he would say, "Was this matter considered by the Official Committee?"

"Yes, Secretary of State," would come the reply. "They had very much in mind the important point put by the Under Secretary of State for Scotland and they recommended that the Bill should provide for four large centres in England and one large and one small centre in Scotland, but that provision should be made for additional centres to be provided by means of a statutory instrument if economic circumstances changed.

"Well, that seems fair enough," the Chairman would say "You have got an extra small centre, Teddy, and the promise of more in the future if required." In short the battle had been fought between the officials and a compromise reached.

We would all concur and move on to the next business.

"Well, here we have a most difficult situation", the Chairman would argue.

"The police are demanding a 10 per cent pay rise, but the Treasury insists that we should not settle for more than 9 per cent, because to pay more than 9 per cent would affect the crucial pay talks with civil servants, nurses and teachers. What do colleagues think?"

My advice may have been to remind colleagues that it was important to preserve police morale, as major disturbances were expected in a big industrial dispute on Clydeside. Another colleague, clearly briefed with care, might argue that the problem could perhaps be resolved by giving the police a 9 per cent pay rise and a special extra one per cent specifically related to the extra cost of cleaning their boots. As neither civil servants, nurses nor teachers tended to wear boots, the problem might be resolved without embarrassing other pay talks.

Then there would probably be an intervention from the Treasury Minister indicating that even if the one per cent was used for cleaning boots, the cost to the Treasury would be an extra £56,000,000 in a full year. This would be difficult to manage within the Budget.

After a thoughtful pause, the Chairman might say "Well, couldn't we help the Treasury by recommending that an extra one per cent for cleaning boots should be offered to the police in the next financial year, with 9 per cent this year?"

As the prospect of a boot allowance next year would probably not be in any of the papers provided to the Ministers, and as they could probably come to the opinion that an extra boot allowance next year would maintain police morale high enough to tackle the rioting in Clydeside, there would be just a murmur of agreement.

The Chairman would sum up.

"Clearly, this is an issue of such magnitude that only the Cabinet can decide, but would I be justified in reporting to my Cabinet colleagues that it was the unanimous recommendation of this Committee, that the boot allowance scheme next year be implemented as a means of resolving this problem?"

My reaction, faced with this challenge, might well have been of panic, wondering what the civil servants would say when I reported back this solution, which had not been covered in the notes.

"I am afraid I have no Departmental advice on a boot allowance, Secretary of State, so perhaps I should not commit the Scottish Office."

"No, Teddy", the kindly Chairman would say – "I cannot emphasise too much that it is this Committee of *Ministers* who make decisions. We are not here as spokesmen for our Departments – it is **we** who make the decisions." With a quizzical look at the civil servant on his right, he would say "and I think that it is the duty of Ministers to constantly remind our quite excellent civil servants that this is a Parliamentary democracy, not a Bureaucratic democracy!"

"Hear, hears" would fill the room and I would look acutely embarrassed. "So, it is unanimous, Teddy, is it not?"

"Of course, Secretary of State," I would whisper, and then set out to return to my office, in the certain knowledge that I would advise the civil servants in the Scottish Home Department about what their Lord and Master had agreed to!

The Minister has a lot of work in the House of Commons. He has to answer questions once a fortnight as well as to approve the draft replies to masses of written questions. He has to speak in debates and deal with interventions from critics, and he has to lead the discussions in Standing Committees when Bills are considered.

Ministers also have important political tasks. The loyal party workers also look to Ministers for guidance and inspiration at meetings of Party Groups and conferences, and Ministers are also expected to do their fair share of constituency lunch clubs and meetings in other areas.

They must never forget that their back-bench colleagues look to them to justify and explain their policies to the voters and to reassure their supporters.

Ministers also have to do at least a fair share of TV and Radio appearances. If, when a new policy is announced, or if a crisis arises in their field of responsibility, the Minister is expected to go on the box and tell the people what it is all about.

But where does family and private life fit into all this? This can be a real nightmare for Ministers in particular, and MPs in general. A Minister, for example, works horrendous hours from Monday to Thursday, spends his Friday at the Ministry, finds that his Saturdays are taken up with local surgeries, bazaars and dinners, and even on Sundays, he will probably have to spend a lot of time on reading official papers delivered to his home or in attending policy group meetings which the Government has a nasty habit of arranging on Sundays.

If a Minister is not careful, the family can be squeezed entirely out of his life, and he can wake up some day to realise that his children have grown up and that he has to make appointments in a busy diary to see his wife!

Wives and families often find that they are being shunted into a second league, with their contact with husband and father always having to take second place to Ministerial, Parliamentary and political commitments and engagements.

All of this probably explains why the House of Commons has been described as a marriage wrecker.

In some ways, I believe that MPs have happier marriages if they marry after being in the Commons.

It is a nasty experience for a family, particularly after all the excitement and glamour of an election or by-election, to find that the father who used to come home at 6pm each night, is never at home in the evenings and may be away living in London for most of the week and to return home at weekends pretty shattered with a pile of constituency or political commitments to honour over the weekend. The friendly chap who used to be there to bath the baby, or to help with the children's homework, or even chat about the problems of the day, is suddenly just not there, and the family takes second place to the demands of politics.

Perhaps the greatest danger comes from those MPs who become obsessed with the pursuit of power – perhaps the most corrupting false god that exists. Of course, the same can apply to business and commerce, but somehow the pursuit of power in politics excludes the wife in a way in which the pursuit of business advancement does not. Nothing is sadder than the sight of men in Parliament who have slaved and schemed to make progress up the Ministerial ladder and who are then deprived of all their power in a Cabinet reshuffle, say at the age of 50 or 55, and who find that, apart from the power withdrawal symptoms, they have lost contact with their homes and families, for the simple reason that so much of their time and energy has been directed to the relentless pursuit of power. Looking back over my 41 years in Parliament, I cannot think of many colleagues who have found joy in Ministerial power. Most of them have fallen off the promotion ladder before they have reached the top of it and wandered around like lost sheep, clearly saddened by the fact that their opinions and comments and even their company at lunch tables or in the coffee room are no longer sought after by colleagues or media men. Even the Prime Ministers themselves have usually left office in sadness and with reluctance.

Without the firm and secure base of a loving and caring home, life can be very sad indeed for the person deprived of power and indeed for the many MPs who lose election after election.

I have been astonishingly blessed with my own marriage and family. I met Sheila, my wife, when she was the social worker in the Westminster Hospital where I had been taken after a collapse following several all night sittings. Had I not had this medical problem, I would probably have been a crusty old bachelor today, because the opportunity for courting is very restricted in Parliament, apart from the very small minority who indulge in womanising in London as a pastime between Parliamentary votes!

Apart from the happy period when I was out of Parliament for a year in 1979 and early 1980 – a break which was more acceptable because I got a good job within two days of my election defeat – life in Parliament has been our style of life. Sheila has carried the main burden of looking after the family, plus the host of constituency and other responsibilities, including taking all these phone calls at home and reporting them to me in our regular phone calls. An essential ingredient in a good marriage, where the husband is on non-stop call, is to pencil in a few weekends in the year when the whole family can just go away to stay with friends or go to a nice hotel and to avoid the temptation of leaving a phone number.

Not only is Sheila a wonderful wife and a lovely companion in marriage, but she is my best political adviser – frequently counselling me against some of the daft ideas which MPs get in their heads from time to time.

Of course we cannot generalise, but I do believe, on the basis of experience over the years, that the silliest thing for an MP to do is regard his family as the second priority of his life, with politics and power as the first – and to regard being an MP or Minister as anything more grand than being an interesting and demanding job, no different in practice from the multitude of jobs done by others.

Mrs Thatcher, when she came to visit us during an election;
behind me is Bernard Braine

16

Opposition and the Shadow Cabinet

The Opposition has a highly important role to play in Parliament. It is the body which questions and criticises government policy and keeps Ministers on their toes by exposing injustices and scandals, and by ventilating in public, the arguments against particular policies.

But the Opposition is also the alternative Government and has the task of preparing the policies which it would apply, if re-elected to power at an election.

The Opposition has to do this, of course, without the whole army of civil servants to provide advice which is available to Ministers. The Opposition front bench team also has the major task of persuading, or seeking to persuade the electorate, through their pronouncements and statements in public, that the Opposition could carry on the task of government more effectively and more justly than the Government in power.

One of my most exciting periods in Parliament was to be in Margaret Thatcher's Shadow Cabinet from late 1976 until 1979 when she prepared the policies which were to be the basis of her period as Prime Minister from 1979.

I would like to think that it was my ability and political fire power that led to my appointment as Shadow Trade spokesman (with Cecil Parkinson as my Shadow Assistant) in November 1976, but I have the feeling that the main reason for my appointment was that Mrs Thatcher wanted a Scottish voice in the Shadow Cabinet to argue against the pro-devolution views of the then Scottish Shadow Minister, Alick

Buchanan Smith, and supported by Francis Pym who was then a most powerful member of the Shadow Cabinet.

The voice did count because while in Ministerial Committees and Cabinets in Government, spokesmen tend to speak only to their own departments, discussions in the Shadow Cabinet tend to be free for alls with spokesmen on foreign affairs feeling perfectly entitled to voice views on farming in Wales, and spokesmen on health feeling that their views on housing were just as important as the housing spokesmen.

Since Ted Heath had committed the Conservative Party in 1970 to devolution, i.e. the provision of separate Parliaments for Scotland and Wales, at which elected assemblymen could make decisions on Scottish laws and Scottish affairs, the Tory Party in Scotland had been divided on the issue. Most Scottish Tories were loyalists and would have supported the leader if she had proposed the establishment of a separate Parliament for Dundee, but there was a deep and rising tide of dissatisfaction amongst some Tories about a prospect which they believed would undermine the unity of the United Kingdom. Others were worried about excessive government, and perhaps even more did not like the idea of what would probably be a permanent socialist administration in a Scottish Parliament.

On the other hand, there were equally strong views by the pro-devolutionists who believed that only a commitment to a separate Parliament for Scotland could effectively put an end to the substantial and apparently increasing support for the Scottish National Party who supported a wholly independent Scotland.

There was also a geographical divide in Scotland with the Tories in the East of Scotland and the "establishment" favouring devolution, and the more brutal and industrial orientated Tories of the West regarding devolution as a costly nonsense. They argued that you could not pacify the SNP with a half-way house, and that the only way of beating them was a head on battle from the Unionist standpoint.

In some ways, the argument represented the divide between the Heathite policies and the Thatcherite policies – with the Heath people believing that a sensible and agreeable compromise was the best way of solving problems, while the Thatcherites believed in fighting their own corner against the enemy.

Devolution was an integral part of the Party's programme, but there were at least signs that Mrs Thatcher did not like the idea and she may have felt that it was better to have a Scot in the Shadow Cabinet putting the case against devolution rather than having the English apparently arguing "against Scotland" as the pro-devolutionists would have put it.

Some also argued at the time that she wanted to school along a possible replacement for Alick Buchanan Smith, who was said to take a moderate and gentlemanly approach to political issues, while she may have preferred to have a harder and more abrasive person to take on the Labour Opposition in Parliament.

Whatever the reason, I was appointed as the Conservative spokesman on trade – an issue on which I had little knowledge at all.

There were clearly dangers to the Party in appointing someone to the Trade Department job who had well known anti-Common Market views and I very much doubt if Mrs Thatcher would have risked putting me into any office in that area when the Party came to power. However we will never know, because after only a month, Alick resigned from the Shadow Cabinet over his sincere doubts on the Leadership's commitment to devolution and Mrs Thatcher asked me to take his place as Scottish spokesman and to promote our Scottish policies, which still included a commitment to devolution.

It is not the first time that Ministers or Shadow spokesmen have had to justify, in public, views which they did not hold, but with the messages from the Shadow Cabinet and my own views, our commitment to devolution became a little less credible every day, despite the constant efforts of Francis Pym to remind the Shadow Cabinet and Party, of the nature of the commitment we had.

So I was charged with the task of organising the Scottish Parliamentary group in Opposition in Parliament and to give a political lead to the Scottish Tory organisation. Meetings of the Shadow Cabinet were fascinating. We spent hours of discussion on what line the Party should take on issues. Whether we should oppose or support Bills or statements coming from the Government, and most important, perhaps, the subjects we should select for debate, drafting policies for a future Conservative Government, and the reports of these committees were invariably reported to the Shadow Cabinet and discussed.

It has been argued over recent years that Mrs Thatcher likes to surround herself with those who agree with her. This was certainly not my experience of the Shadow Cabinet. For a start, it would not have helped Party unity if the so-called moderates had felt that they did not have representatives in the Shadow Cabinet. Moreover, Mrs Thatcher's process of decision-making appeared to require disagreement.

She would put an argument – for example, she might propose that we should vote against a Labour Bill to control council rents, on the grounds that this would mean higher rate rises. Somebody, often Jim Prior, Geoffrey Howe or Frances Pym would put the contrary view and argue the case fiercely in terms of what the impact of such a decision might be on potential Tory voters and on our freedom of action in a future Conservative Government. There was an invariable pattern to these discussions.

The argument would proceed and if it appeared that Mrs Thatcher was getting the best of the argument, a decision would be made to support her. If she seemed to be losing the argument on the basis of facts or logic, Willie Whitelaw would intervene with an almost tearful appreciation of the importance and significance of the Thatcher case, but would argue that in view of the obvious complexities of the case and the need to obtain further information about its consequences, there might be merit in referring the whole issue to a sub-committee or to a group of experts in our Conservative Research Department for detailed study. These study reports rarely, if ever appeared to come back to the Shadow Cabinet, but with his unique healing touch, Willie prevented Mrs Thatcher appearing to be defeated.

My assessment of individuals changed remarkably within the Shadow Cabinet. I had always regarded Jim Prior as an anti-Thatcherite and Heathite campaigner, but I learned through time that he was perhaps the most loyal and decent member of the team. He would argue fiercely against Mrs Thatcher's views, but once the decision had been arrived at, he would give total support and he never engaged in the scheming or plotting which some of his colleagues did in a most disloyal way.

Then there were the power seekers who clearly regarded Mrs Thatcher – as they would any leader – as the person blocking their path to the top job and would spend much of their time seeking to build up personal support. I can recall one member of the Shadow Cabinet – who I knew had a wholehearted distaste for me and my views – going out of his way to tell me, when walking away from a meeting, that he wished to congratulate me on the powerful argument I had made and on the most effective way in which I had presented it. This was followed by a suggestion that sensible people like himself and myself in the Shadow Cabinet were getting a bit worried about the way in which Mrs Thatcher was steering policy and would I like to come to his home for a chat about it, over lunch. I might have been impressed had I not known that he homed in on a different member of the Shadow team after every meeting to put the same tributes and invitations in an almost identical way.

I also saw how reputations were made. One Member of the team was almost universally regarded as being the wisest member of the Shadow Cabinet because he always looked wise and rarely said anything about anything.

I do not think that at any stage I made an enormous impact on the Shadow Cabinet. Amongst my many faults, I have a weakness of making outrageous and impractical suggestions at meetings of slightly pompous people, and I think that it caused some little irritation when during a discussion on agricultural policy I made the suggestion - which in fairness had a logical and economic base – that the next Conservative Government should discourage the practice of agriculture.

However, they had to put up with me, because devolution was obviously a key issue in Parliament

– the issue which was eventually to bring down the Callaghan Government – and I appeared to be the only Scottish Tory under 60 years of age who was willing to wage war on the Socialist plans to set up devolved Parliaments.

It would be cruel and unfair to former colleagues to mention any of the debates which we had on policy, but suffice to say that my principal contribution was to establish in Scotland a major and effective task force to battle against the devolution plans in the Referendum campaign which the Government initiated in Scotland, and to lead the "Keep Britain United" and "Scotland says No" campaign, although a goodly number of active Conservatives and Scottish Conservative MPs were active in the "Yes for Scotland" campaign.

Our campaign was based on bashing devolution head on, despite the rather frantic activity in the Shadow Cabinet of Francis Pym, our constitutional spokesman, to get the campaign more based on the idea that we opposed the Labour devolution plan but would bring forward a better and more acceptable Conservative devolution plan. The referendum campaign was great fun and although there was a small majority for devolution in the referendum, the supporters got nothing like the 40 per cent of Scottish votes which the Government required to implement its plan. Strange to say, although we actually lost the battle, the general view in Parliament and amongst most of the public was that we had won. In the sense that we had blocked the plans, I suppose victory was ours, and we had also achieved success, in that the almost overwhelming support for devolution, at the beginning of the campaign, was eroded to a highly marginal degree of support.

The Government which had a tiny majority in Parliament, suffered a defeat on a motion of confidence shortly after the Referendum, because the minority parties – like the Scottish and Welsh nationalists – voted against Jim Callaghan when it became clear that the Government was not to proceed with its devolution plans.

I think the result of the 1979 election in Scotland showed that the Conservatives had been at least politically wise to oppose devolution instead of going along with it. The Scottish Nationalists, who had been experiencing soaring support and had seized a large number of the traditional Tory seats – were slaughtered in that election and the Tories made huge gains, and Mrs Thatcher was swept to power, partly because of the devolution crusade which lost Labour its Nationalist support in Parliament. We had been able to force an election at a time when the Government didn't want it, and we achieved this because Labour lost its Nationalist support in Parliamentary votes with the devolution issue going the wrong way for them.

I have always had a sneaking feeling of satisfaction and achievement that if I had not been successful in leading the great campaign against the Callaghan devolution plans in Scotland, the General Election might have been delayed for a few months and Mrs Thatcher might not have been the Prime Minister. However, on the other hand, my feelings of achievement have to be tempered by the obvious fact that politicians have an incurable habit of overestimating their own importance and significance!

While 1979 was a joyous time for the Tories both North and South of the Border, it was a personal disaster for me. I lost my seat in Cathcart – one of the very few election losses that year. There were two reasons – or perhaps three. First, the slow but steady deterioration in the constituency had caught up with me – like all the city seats, we were losing our staunch middle class support as the residents moved out to the suburbs. Second, I had cooked my own goose with my campaign against the Nationalists. The slump in the SNP vote gained us many seats in Scotland, but in Cathcart, the same slump in SNP support simply boosted the Labour vote, because in the West, Nationalist voters tended to come from traditional Labour ranks while in the East, they tended to come from former Tories. And thirdly, in fairness, the Labour Party in Glasgow put a huge effort in to the campaign, bussing loads of active Party workers into Cathcart and Castlemilk to achieve one of the most effective campaigns I have ever seen. While they were doing this – with the obvious objective of securing the prize of defeating the Tory Shadow Secretary – I was spending much of my time travelling round Scotland and supporting candidates in the key marginal seats, and perhaps there was a bit of complacency in my own election team, who, having seen me survive against all odds and prophecies in three elections, assumed wrongly that I was unbeatable.

However, beaten I was, and instead of joining the Government as Secretary of State for Scotland and a Member of the Cabinet, I was out of Parliament and out of a job, with a wife and three children to support.

After the by-election, looking for a house with the family

17

In the wilderness

I have always taken the view that good comes out
of every situation if you look for it, and I am in no
doubt that my defeat in Cathcart and my exclusion
in consequence from the dizzy heights of Ministerial
advancement was a great blessing in many ways. If
I had won, I would have faced a real nightmare of
non-stop horrendous work, just at a time when my
young children were growing up, and there could
have been no security because it was sadly obvious
that there was no security for a Tory in Cathcart.
Even though the boundaries were greatly improved
after the 1979 election, Labour has held the seat
ever since with increased majorities and Cathcart
has joined the long string of city seats like Pollok,
Craigton, Scotstoun and even affluent Hillhead,
where the Conservatives have lost control.

I therefore decided that I would not return
to politics at all unless I was able to secure a seat
within travelling distance of London so that I could
spend more time with the family. The prospects of
persuading a constituency in the South to adopt, as
a candidate, a Scotsman with a clear Scottish accent,
were limited. As in any event the next election was
clearly years away, I determined to settle down to
a normal life and to obtain a normal job, but what
job is an ex-MP qualified to do?

I had an approach within a day from a public
relations company in the South who clearly
were looking for someone with the knowledge of
Parliamentary processes and personal contacts with
MPs who could help to out their clients' causes
to MPs and Ministers. However, the prospect of

spending my time making use of goodwill with former colleagues to invite them to lunches with clients and sending them circulars which would end up in their waste paper baskets, just did not appeal, and in any event it would have meant moving to London, which was not very attractive, bearing in mind that house prices there were horrific and that our whole lives had been in Glasgow with the children now happily settled in school there.

So, with the solitary security of a cheque for two months pay from Parliament (the then redundancy payment after 15 years employment) I began to wonder how I could support the family. I had not been able to save any money and the prospects looked grim.

However, the good news came soon.

The Editor of the Sunday Mail – one of Scotland's leading popular newspapers – invited me to write a punchy weekly column for this paper which was part of the Mirror Group. For this service, I was offered a yearly contract which gave me almost as much income as I had received as an MP.

To boost my income more I had an invitation from a leading engineering group in England who asked me to be their political adviser for a useful annual fee. I tried, after my appointment, to give a service to the company by sending them little summaries of my assessment of the political scene and I called down from time to time to have meetings with them. However, they constantly advised me not to trouble too much because what they wanted was to have someone they could call on if they wanted advice.

To this day, I do not have the slightest idea of what my job was meant to be, and I have a deep down feeling that some colleagues or former colleagues in Parliament had suggested to the company that poor old Teddy Taylor would have a problem supporting his family and that it would help if he could be given a little job which presumably would not be terribly important within the Company's huge resources. I never really discovered the origin of my appointment or indeed what I was actually meant to do, but if, as I suspect, it was just a kindly gesture, I can only offer my thanks to my anonymous benefactor. Finally, my income was secured by the fact that my MP colleague and closest personal friend, Richard Shepherd, whose grocery company Board was my only business activity apart from being an MP, advised me out of the blue, that the Board had decided to increase the directors' salaries.

All these things being taken into account, our family finances were secure and I was able to enjoy the immense luxury of leading my own life and not having huge sections of my time belonging to others.

So I settled down to the non-political life and enjoyed it immensely.

But within twelve months, an unexpected opportunity arose. The MP for South West Herts died and it seemed that this would indeed be the kind of seat which could get me back to Parliament and was near enough to London to enable me to have contact with the family and not be away all week.

So I sent in a detailed application, describing all my talents and experience. However in reply, I received a brief note indicating that I was not really the chap they were looking for and there was no need for me to call even for an interview.

Having received such a frosty response, Sheila and I concluded that there was no prospect of returning to Parliament. The opportunities in Scotland were very limited – with most of the Tory seats being in the East with healthy MPs who seemed certain to live for a very long time. If the English would not even look at me, the door seemed closed.

Within a few weeks however, there was a vacancy in Southend East because of the tragic death of the sitting Member, Sir Stephen McAdden, in an accident.

Was it worth while bothering to even apply?

I was actually travelling to London to have a chat and a cup of tea with Mrs Thatcher, who despite her hectic life as Premier, always went out of her way to show an interest in former colleagues who had fallen on hard political times. I think that there are many who would testify that this great lady, who is represented as being tough and unfeeling, has a heart of gold. As it was my first trip back to London since my defeat, I took Sheila with me and while she went to do some shopping, I called to see the Prime Minister.

When I explained to her the cold reception I had had from the Hertfordshire Tories and suggested that I would be giving up politics, the PM insisted that I had to keep trying and she reminded me that she herself had visited many constituency associations and received many snubs before she had eventually been selected as candidate for Finchley.

Heartened by this exhortation, Sheila and I paid a visit to Southend, which was only an hour from London, and we immediately fell in love with it.

It seemed to be the ideal constituency in every way. It was not agricultural for a start (my EEC views would have been difficult to sell to farmers), it was a busy and bustling place containing many East-Enders from London who had "made good" and it was clearly a delightful place to live and to bring up a family.

I had prepared, before the visit, a short letter of application. We went into Franco's restaurant for a meal and I sealed the envelope and posted it in Nelson Street, just beside the Tory HQ. I often wonder if the Southend Tories wondered why the applicant from Scotland had posted his letter in Nelson Street, Southend.

There were hundreds of applicants and there were several interviews. Clearly, there were some who doubted the wisdom of selecting a Scotsman, and of course I did not know the nature of the private discussions.

However, from what I have heard since, it was Sheila who got the seat for me. The key factor appeared to be the interview of wives, and all the wives were asked if, in the event of their husbands being adopted and elected, they would play a part in the activities of the women Conservatives.

One of the wives apparently assured the questioners that she would play a very active part, and being a splendid organiser would ensure that their women's branch would become the most powerful and effective one in the area. Sheila, however, explained that she could not play a very active part, as her main responsibility would be looking after her husband and young family, but that she would be delighted to come along to attend functions organised by the Ladies. This response seemed to be infinitely more acceptable than the prospect of the intense and dominating enthusiast who was going to sort them all out, and so I was selected by a majority which I think was less than the newspapers suggested.

So we had the by-election. It was really about the nastiest I have ever taken part in. Although there was a 10,000 majority, the Government was rather unpopular and the Tory candidate from Scotland was particularly unpopular.

A lot of local people understandably asked why on earth the local Party could not find a candidate anywhere in Essex or even England, and if they had to go to Scotland for one, why did they have to go to Glasgow which seemed to be a wholly different place from Southend.

The popular Labour candidate was a local man and it was a fair point that he knew a great deal more about Southend and its problems than a Scot who had never even visited the place before the by-election had been called.

The Liberals ran a particularly nasty campaign with a series of spiteful and, at least in my opinion, wholly unjustified personal attacks.

However I had a grand election team to help and reassure me, a magnificent agent produced by our Central Office and also a team of Scots who took the trouble to come down to Southend to help my campaign.

It was a neck and neck contest and I scraped through with a majority of only 400, but – as Mrs Thatcher stated – one was enough, and within two months our family had moved down to Southend *en bloc*, rather to the chagrin of the Liberals who had stated that I would be living in Scotland and that Mrs Thatcher had "set up the seat" for me so that I could be one of her Scottish Ministers.

It has proved to be a very happy move. When the General Election came along, I found that I had been accepted as a Southender and the majority returned to 10,000.

Like Cathcart, it is a busy and demanding constituency and like Cathcart, the residents are kindly and appreciative. Unlike Cathcart, it is near enough to London for me to travel back home on quite a few nights to sleep in my own bed and to see the children in the mornings before school.

My life has been haunted with luck.

18

The Christian dimension

There can be few people, whether motivated by faith or without faith, who do not think deeply at some stage about the purpose of their lives and of their work or service. Do we have, as individuals, a duty to make a specific contribution to life on our planet, the existence and purpose of which has been such an enigma to all those without a perfect faith or an unquestioning mind?

Because the teachings of the Bible point us in the direction of loving our neighbours, caring for the poor and handicapped and upholding the moral code of the Commandments, Christians through the ages have questioned whether their church and their believers have a special role in using the political system as a means of "getting things done" in these areas of human concern.

The issue, which nowadays is referred to as the Church and Politics, is one, which has perplexed and divided Christians from the earliest days.

When the Christian faith was given approval and even encouragement by the Emperor Constantine, it is recorded that Christians in positions of authority, met together, and no doubt prayed together, to determine whether there was a particular approach to the business of Government, which Christians should adopt. However it is also recorded that St Anthony took a group of his followers into the wilds of the Egyptian desert to free them from the corrupting influences of the temporal world and to enable them to concentrate on the saving of their souls.

We find in the Middle Ages, temporal rulers and monarchs were instructed by church leaders to use

PLEASE DISPLAY IN WINDOW OR CAR

TEDDY TAYL

CONSERVATI

Published by R. F. Nelder, 16 Nelson Street, Southend

Introdu

Following the sad death o
long serving M.P. Sir S
TEDDY TAYLOR has bee
the by-election on March 1
Teddy Taylor offers you:

EXPERIENCE He has
for fifteen years, has
Government Minister, and
Shadow Cabinet.

COMMITMENT Even hi
have recognised that the
conscientious M.P.'s in
constituency duties an
constituents' interests.

Published by R. F. Nelder, 16 Nelson Street, Souther

Details of Teddy Taylor's campaign and Public Meetings will be available from his Campaign Headquarters at 16 Nelson Street, Southend. Tel: Southend 46264

Printed by the Apollo Press, Southchurch Road, Southend

cing Teddy
Taylor

f Southend East's
ephen McAdden,
n selected to fight
th.

erved as an M.P.
>een a successful
a member of the

political opponents
e were few more
attending to his
l protecting his

YOUR CONSERVATIVE CANDIDATE

PRINCIPLE   He has shown on many occasions that he placed principle before career—for example when he resigned a Government Ministry because of his personal opposition to Britain joining the E.E.C.

PERSONALITY   He is a family man with three young children and is active in church and youth work. He has the sincerity and friendliness which Southend East expects from its M.P. and will live here with his family.

and Printed by the Apollo Press, Southchurch Road, Southend.

the resources and power of the state to persecute sects like the Catharians whose beliefs and practices were not in line with the then teachings of the "official church". Likewise the Spanish Inquisition took the view that the civil powers had a duty to co-operate in the elimination of persons who were not regarded, by their tests, as being true believers.

There were some, like the great John Calvin, who took the view that the Church should not only influence politics, but take over the mechanism of government as a whole, and so he established his "saintly city" of Geneva where the Church authorities are recorded as providing their own law courts and of trying and condemning poor citizens for crimes like, "swearing", "dancing" and saying "that the Pope was a good man" and for blaming the increase in inflation on the influx of Hugenot refugees.

In Britain we had the experience of that remarkable man, Oliver Cromwell, who chopped the king's head off and proceeded to experiment with a whole series of constitutional alternatives including his "Assembly of Saints". Having become distressed by the bickering of politicians, he resolved to gather together all the good Christian folk, who, he hoped, would pass and implement Godly laws. He had a battle on his hands however with the Levellers who believed that the only hope for society was the revoking of strong central power and the equalisation of wealth.

Today we have a rising number of clerics who believe that the Church should be actively involved in the business of politics, to produce political programmes and to issue political statements of policy, while we have other Christians, like Jehovah's Witnesses and the Close Brethren who feel that Christians should not even participate in the business of politics because to do so is usurping

The successful election contest in Southend beside one of my opponents, Humphrey Berkeley

God's rule of the world which he achieves through his mighty powers.

Of course, there are very few churchmen who would seek to argue that Christians should be instructed to vote for particular political parties but there is a large and growing group who takes the view that the church has a clear duty to give advice on great issues of principle, like the harbouring of nuclear weapons, the maintenance of apartheid and the need to expand welfare programmes and foreign aid. The Church, they argue, must speak out on these great issues and give a lead to the decision- makers.

My own view is that it is wrong, divisive and contrary to the teachings of the gospel for the Church, as a body, to associate itself with particular policies. On the other hand, I think that scripture guides us to the conclusions that individual Christians, with their responsibility for their fellow men, should be involved in politics and should seek to use their talents in this area of human activity.

Why so?

For a start, I doubt if there is any political issue which I have encountered in my political career which I believe would readily be regarded as having wholly wrong or absolutely right answers, and I can think of no issue in which persons have not taken alternative views each for good and thoughtful motives.

The conduct of war? There are some who would argue that it is inconceivable that any Christian could participate in war because it involves the killings of innocents and of fellow human beings. However it is not as easy as that. If, in 1939, Britain had not declared war against Germany and had allowed the Germans to invade our nation, would we not have had a personal responsibility for the

Walking the longest pier in the world in Southend with the family.

Opening the premises in Southend

deaths of the 500,000 or so Jews in our country who would have been sent to the gas chambers?

Capital punishment? Again, there are those who say that it is impossible for a Christian to support a measure which results in the deliberate killing of a human for the crime of murder, but if a Christian is convinced, on the basis of available evidence that the maintenance of capital punishment can deter a significant number of murderers, does he not have any responsibility for the deaths of the innocents murdered in the absence of a deterrent?

Foreign Aid? Again, there are many who claim that it is an essential Christian duty for the more affluent states to give substantial sums in aid to the poorer ones. There will be some who argue that the track record of aid programmes shows no material or long-term benefit to poor nations and that it is a greater service to underdeveloped countries to promote free trade and provide a market on which the poor countries can build up wealth creating industries and businesses. It is not unique for politicians one day to call for more foreign aid and the next, to call for the imposing of tough protection against imports from poor countries.

Experiments on animals? Again there are some who claim that no Christian could justify the deliberate torture and ill treatment of innocent animals for experimentation, but others argue that with such experiments, new cures and drugs which alleviate human suffering, are made possible.

Nuclear weapons? Again some argue that no Christian could ever contemplate spending scarce resources on the manufacture of horrendous weapons of mass destruction. Others argue that the existence of such weapons of mass destruction deters aggressors and prevents wars.

There always seem to be two sides to every issue with genuine people disagreeing for genuine reasons.

But apart from this aspect of the matter, I see grave dangers in churches taking a political stance because the inevitable result is political churches. I am told, although I do not know, that in South Africa, people who support apartheid tend to go to the Dutch Reformed Church, people who oppose it attend the Anglican Church, and those who are undecided tend to go to the Presbyterian Churches. It may be a fable, but there can be little doubt that the political stances taken by some churches on both sides of the Atlantic have tended to give them political tags, and such tags can, I believe, serve no other purpose than alienating those who disagree, and diverting people from the spreading of the gospels.

For most Christians, the greatest guidance is from Scripture itself, and we see from Scripture that Christ was challenged to take political stances on several occasions. Perhaps the most direct was when he was challenged to say if it was lawful for citizens of Israel to pay taxes to the illegal colonial regime which was in control of their country, and we can recall his answer that we had a duty to render to Caesar what was Caesar's and to God what was God's.

The message I take from this is that the only circumstances in which the organised church has a duty to speak out on a political issue is when the mechanisms of the State are used to curb or deny the freedom to preach the word or to worship.

I can find no justification in Scripture for the Church to pursue particular political solutions or for them to expect Christian folk to join in social crusades.

Remembering the story about the woman who was caught in the act of adultery and whom Christ was invited to condemn, I feel that the guidance we have is to do things and to fight for issues for the right motive.

There are many policies, which can be supported by people for wholly different motives. I can think of a colleague who supports immigration controls because he believes deeply that the removal of controls would disturb good relations between races in our nation, but I can think of another who supported exactly the same policy for what appeared to be the securing of support and votes from people with prejudices.

In short, it is the motive for supporting the policy and not the policy itself, which should activate all with a faith.

Is the policy being supported because there is a genuine belief that it will help humanity, or is it being supported or opposed because it will be agreeable to voters or easy to explain or defend?

At the end of the day, we all have to live with our consciences and ourselves. We can learn and benefit from errors of judgement, but there is nothing to be gained or secured from a decision made for unworthy or thoughtless motives.

Perhaps one of the most basic Christian duties we have is to be grateful for our blessings.

I am in no doubt that one of our greatest blessings in Britain is the form of democratic Government, which has built up over the years and has endured. There are few places in the world where men and women can be so free and yet be so effectively governed through a system, which provides justice and security.

Playing a very small part in the business of government is a unique privilege, of which I know that every Member and former Member of our Parliament is keenly aware.

19

Is it all worthwhile?

But what can actually be achieved as a Member of Parliament? Can you use your talent to persuade Governments and political parties to change their minds? And what advice should we give to those wishing to take up politics in the future?

I think that the first clear message to convey is that in every constituency there is a crying need for help from the people who feel that they have been unfairly dealt with by the massive bureaucracy of national and local government and who feel wholly unable to present their case through the facilities available to them. A satisfactory MP would be a person who gets to know all the departments well, who fights hard to ensure that those working there get a fair deal and who establishes personal relationships so that a genuine case of unfairness or neglect can receive urgent attention. The other necessity is to be available to constituents who wish to call for a chat and the weekly surgery, which offers appointments, is the best arrangement. If you are going to do the job well for constituents, it is important that you should get to know all the departments and in particular to establish clear and acceptable procedures for communication.

Most MPs I believe, receive a substantial number of enquiries from constituents by letter, phone calls or surgery visits and almost all of them require to be passed on to departments so their replies can be secured. In this connection, it is important that the MP should establish a form of enquiry when he believes that there is a genuine case of neglect or injustice. My experience has always been that so long as you play straight and fair with departments and give them credit and appreciation when they respond well, you can secure the right remedy for protecting constituents.

What is also just as vital for constituents is to have an effective way of communicating with them and of clarifying exactly what you are seeking to do for them.

Over my 41 years in Parliament I had a whole series of secretaries who did a great job for me but the vital factor was to have a second secretary who was willing to work over weekends. The normal arrangement I had for surgeries was to have it on a Saturday morning, to see around 20 people, to stay on for an hour or two to dictate letters to the callers and to the appropriate department, to place the tapes on my desk and then to let the secretary know that all was well. She would come in on the Saturday afternoon or Sunday morning, would deliver my mail to my home, we would then sign and post the mail so that everyone who called on a Saturday would get a letter on Monday morning summarising the issues we had discussed and then endeavouring to clarify exactly what I was seeking to do and when I would expect to be getting a reply.

Arrangements like this can be time consuming, can involve a great deal of effort and some rushing if you are having to go and speak at a dinner on the Saturday night. But genuinely, it is an arrangement which brings satisfaction to constituents, who often feel that nobody cares about them, that their problems are serious and that nobody is willing to give them any priority.

While constituents do deserve speedy and effective action by their elected representatives, it is also just as important for everyone that the MPs should have a comprehensive understanding of what burdens and problems are being encountered by the departments and the range of problems which they are seeking to deal with. Of course it is always possible for a politician to secure the short term boost of a headline in the local press by bashing alleged incompetence by departments. However short term boosts never really help in solving problems, and one of the great failures of politicians in all parties is their unwillingness to appreciate that many of the serious problems facing government and local departments stem directly from the laws and regulations passed by politicians.

So, is the answer just to get a nice reply for constituents? Far from it. Of course it often does help to have a well argued and comprehensive reply, signed by the head of a department, explaining to a constituent why decisions which they object to have to be applied, but the real bonus for an MP is being able to sort out an injustice and resolve a problem. All MPs could give examples.

As I think about it, two examples come to mind. The first was a greatly concerned father who considered that his son, who was facing eviction because of a change in rent entitlement arrangements, might commit suicide. Happily in a few days, I was able to establish that his son's tenancy had started much earlier, which meant that he was able to establish that the son could secure an additional £15 in weekly benefits. It was a real joy to clarify the position to the father.

I can also recall a young man who was being sent back to Zimbabwe because he was not undertaking what was classified as adequate education at one of our local colleges. I was able to initiate an appeal on the basis that the rules did not apply to university education, that the college in question had part of a university included in it and that the young man participated in these arrangements. The persons hearing the appeal in London could not have been more courteous and I think that they soon accepted that the case was genuine and not a fiddle. It would be difficult to describe how pleased I was to advise my young constituent, who seemed reconciled to failure, that we had won the case, to take him for an afternoon tea at a lovely hotel in the Strand and then to stand beside him when he telephoned his father in Zimbabwe to explain that what he referred to as the "High Court of Appeal" had been a great victory.

All MPs could give a multitude of such cases, The important issue is, of course, that in a democracy, it is vital that there should be someone available to help in putting forward appeals for justice and fair play. Just as important for the democracy is that the public representative must be directly answerable to the people in elections. If we change over to the undemocratic nonsense of proportional representation, similar to what we have in the European Parliament elections, it simply means that the real power is switched from the people to the political parties.

But should MPs not work as well or with as much commitment for their voters if they have been selected by the local party bosses? It would be wonderful if that was the case, but sadly when the people only have the right to select a party and when the vast majority of voters haven't a clue who their PR representatives are, the commitment to work for the people simply fades away.

Of course there are always two sides to an argument and I have to admit that MPs working well under the traditional system can sometimes be given unfair credit for their endeavours. I will never forget a lady who called at my surgery, who explained that she had approached everyone and every department about the scandal of her street light not working for a long time; and she had come to me as a last resort. She phoned my home on the Saturday night to say that I was wonderful, that my endeavours had confirmed her support for me and that the lights were now working. When I tried to explain that my surgery letters had not yet been posted, she rejected my explanation by saying that she had heard from others that I was humble and unwilling to take credit for my achievements!

ELECTION SPECIAL

SIR TEDDY TAYLOR
the right champion for Southend East

IT IS TWELVE YEARS since Southend East chose Teddy Taylor to be its Member of Parliament.

Elected with a wafer-thin majority of four hundred he promised then to fight for all the people in the constituency and to battle for the borough in Parliament.

Since then he has served the community so well that at the last election in 1987 his majority was almost 14,000—the highest ever in the history of the constituency.

Teddy's record is one of impeccable service to the constituency.

A family man with local interests, he spends much time in the borough meeting constituents and helping to solve their problems.

Dedication

But at the same time he never neglects his duties in the House of Commons, ensuring that your interests are always well represented.

His dedication has not gone unnoticed and the knighthood received in the last Honours List is a just reward for a man who has given so much unstinting service to his constituents.

Now democracy requires that you elect again a representative for Southend East in Westminster!

Vote Taylor again !

He's the right man to fight for us all. The right man for the job.

Sometimes the telephone never seems to stop ringing ! However, Teddy finds it an invaluable way of keeping in touch and ensuring that he is always kept up-to-date with what is going on in the constituency.

TEDDY TAYLOR lives in Southend with his wife and family. He keeps in touch with his constituents.

TEDDY TAYLOR attends the office in Southchurch Road to meet and talk to any of his constituents who wish to see him, working tirelessly to resolve their problems. Last year alone he had over 1,400 interviews with constituents.

TEDDY TAYLOR receives about 10,000 letters each year — he answers them all personally.

TEDDY TAYLOR visits old folk's clubs, church organisations, schools and factories throughout the constituency, meeting you, the people.

TEDDY TAYLOR speaks up for Southend in Parliament to ensure a fair deal for you and the borough. He gets results !

TEDDY TAYLOR takes in the region of a thousand residents on tours of Parliament each year—women's groups, pensioners and school-children.

1992, April

No one was more surprised than Teddy when he received a knighthood in the Honours List. These usually go to "well behaved" long-servers in Westminster and Teddy has a reputation for having an independent mind. However, everyone agreed it was a fitting recognition of years of hard work for the constituents he represents. He is pictured above with wife Sheila and sons John and George at the Palace.

ABOVE LEFT: Accepting a cheque at the Conservative Club for a children's charity.
ABOVE RIGHT: The family man—at home with wife Sheila and daughter Louise.
BELOW: Enjoying lunch with pupils at Cecil Jones Secondary School.

Postal votes and proxies

THOSE who are sick, on holiday or away from home in connection with their employment can obtain postal or proxy votes.

Remember, it is your right to be able to vote, so don't miss this opportunity as your vote could be vital.

But time is short—so don't delay. Telephone Teddy Taylor's Committee Rooms Southend 600460 for advice.

ON THURSDAY APRIL 9th 1992 — VOTE FOR

TAYLOR TEDDY X
—the right man for Southend East

WHERE DOES TEDDY STAND?

TEDDY TAYLOR is well known for his strong and outspoken views on many of the most important issues affecting the country generally and his constituents in particular. Many major national and local issues have recently surfaced and we set out the standpoint Teddy has taken and will continue to take if given another term of office.

BLOODSPORTS

He is opposed to hunting wild animals with hounds and was one of the sponsors of the recent Bill in Parliament which sought to abolish fox-hunting.

SOUTHEND UNITED

Teddy is a "regular" at Roots Hall and has stated he will do everything in his power to keep Southend United within the borough.

THE PIER

He's an enthusiast for the Pier and President of the Pier Society.

His pressure helped to secure the first ever Government grant for repairs, and he supports enthusiastically the new investment plan by the Miller family, of Peter Pan's Playground, to rebuild the end of the Pier and provide new attractions.

THE EUROPEAN COMMUNITY

Teddy has never hidden his opposition to the transfer of power to Brussels and to E.C. spending schemes which he regards as wasteful.

He led the backbench revolt against joining the Exchange Rate Mechanism which he argues prevents interest rate cuts and damages job improvement.

THE ELDERLY

Teddy is a champion of the senior citizens and supports a separate pensioners' indexing of prices to ensure pension rises reflect more accurately the needs of the elderly.

CAN WE SAVE THE GRAMMAR SCHOOLS?

ONE ISSUE on which voters should be in no doubt whatsoever is that the survival of Southend's four grammar schools depends on a Conservative victory in the Election.

Although attended by about a quarter of our secondary school children, Labour has made it quite clear that if they win, all grammar schools will be closed.

Southend High School for Boys and Girls and the Westcliff High Schools, again for boys and girls, offer a unique opportunity for children from all parts of Southend, irrespective of background or income, to receive free grammar school education.

It would be tragic if the freedom of the people of Southend to decide on the structure of the education for our children were to be removed simply on the basis of central Socialist dogma.

But does the existence of grammar schools undermine the other secondary schools?

The evidence is certainly not there from our own experience in Southend where schools like Shoeburyness High and Cecil Jones are providing excellent educational opportunities and results.

Decision

However, even if some still consider this a valid argument, should not the decision be left to the people and the parents of Southend-on-Sea?

If they want to scrap the grammar schools they can elect a council which would do this.

And if they want to retain them they can vote for a Conservative council—as they have.

The decision should be ours —not made for us by Mr. Kinnock and his Socialist team in Whitehall.

Remember that if the grammar schools are scrapped it will be the able children from the poorer homes who would suffer most.

Progress at last on the misery line

TEDDY TAYLOR is demanding action on investment on the notorious Fenchurch Street line.

And he has plagued the transport ministers to come up with cash to alleviate the problems faced daily by the long-suffering commuters in his Southend East constituency.

£260m.

Now B.R. has agreed to a massive £260m. plan to replace the route, the rolling stock and the signalling.

The contract for the new signalling (about £50m.) has now been placed.

Fare rise cut

In recognition of the poor service, Sir Teddy has helped persuade B.R. to cut the fare rise this year by three per cent.

Although this in itself will not improve the service, it will soften the blow to the fare-paying passengers.

"It's great to have these new pledges," says Teddy.

"But I'll not be satisfied until it all happens!"

PHOTO-CALL FOR TEDDY. . .

LEFT: Teddy Taylor is a regular visitor to nursery schools, which he wants to expand. Here he enjoys a dance with a youngster at a new nursery in Westcliff. BELOW: Having fun with youngsters at the Kursaal Community Centre. FOOT OF PAGE: With the teenagers !

As M.P. for the Southend East Constituency Sir Teddy Taylor (pictured above outside the Houses of Parliament), spent more time in the Commons than most other M.P.s, always working for the good of all his constituents, no matter what their political views.

ON THE CAMPAIGN TRAIL

WHERE YOU CAN SEE AND HEAR TEDDY TAYLOR and other prominent speakers   All meetings commence 8 p.m.

TUESDAY, MARCH 24th

SHOEBURYNESS HIGH SCHOOL

Caulfield Road
Shoeburyness

TUESDAY, APRIL 7th

WESTBOROUGH HIGH SCHOOL

Boston Avenue
Southend-on-Sea

MONDAY, APRIL 6th

GREENWAYS JUNIOR SCHOOL

Greenways
Thorpe Bay

WEDNESDAY, APRIL 8th

SOUTHEND HIGH SCHOOL FOR GIRLS

Southchurch Boulevard
Southend-on-Sea

ALL WELCOME   YOUR QUESTIONS ANSWERED

BETTER DEAL FOR SOUTHEND

OVER THE YEARS Southend has received less than other parts of the country in Government grants for the local council.   The argument was that Southend did not have the same problems.

Teddy Taylor fought long and hard to put this right, and last year he won the battle.

That is why when every poll tax payer in the U.K. received a grant of £130, Southend poll tax payers received an extra £69 per head in addition to that £130

That's the main reason why our poll tax of £420 per head fell to just over £200.

And you can rest assured that Teddy will always battle hard to ensure that Southend retains its new "fair" grant allocation.

Health Service cash boost

SOUTHEND has always received less Health Service cash than many other areas.

Happily this injustice has now been resolved.

A new grant system is being phased in over five years—we've now had the first two instalments —and the Southend area will receive an EXTRA sum of between £10m. and £15m.

Again an injustice has been put right.

And Teddy was on hand to perform the opening ceremony when some of this money was used to provide a new Health Service unit in Shoeburyness.

Return to borough status for Southend?

THE NEW Local Government Reform Act which has just been passed by Parliament gives Southend the opportunity of becoming a county borough once again.

A decision is likely to be made in the very near future.

Most Southenders seem to want to return to the situation when the Civic Centre ran all the local services.

Believe it or not, Labour M.P.s all voted against the Bill !

Published by E. W. J. Lockhart, 1 Strand House, 742 Southchurch Road, Southend   Printed by Goodyear Printers, 70 Southchurch Avenue, Southend

1992, April

What about all these conflicting claims by politicians?

I THINK the real problem is not that any party is telling a bunch of untruths but that the WHOLE story is not always being told.

If we look at spending on schools, for example, Labour has claimed that this has been "cut".

It is certainly true that as a percentage of total spending by the nation the share allotted to schools has fallen from 5.3 per cent to 4.6 per cent.

But there are one-and-a-half million fewer pupils in our schools compared with 1979. And national spending has soared.

The facts are that in **cash** terms spending per head in junior and nursery schools has gone up from £430 to £1,325.

So that in real terms, allowing for prices rises, the increase has been forty-one per cent.

For secondary schools the increase per head has been from £605 to over £2,000. In real terms this is an increase of fifty-three per cent.

As a share of our Gross National Product we actually spend **more** on education than either Japan or Germany.

So the next time you hear about a Tory "cut", ask for the full story.

Teddy joins in class work on one of his regular visits to local schools

Hospitals and the Health Service

AT LEAST no one questions that there has been a huge increase in spending in the Health Service. The "real" increase in spending has been fifty-five per cent.

The number of doctors and dentists increased by 17,000.

The number of nurses and midwives has increased by 69,000.

Hospitals are treating over a million more patients a year as in-patients and over two million more a year as out-patients.

There has been a reform to establish Trusts to ensure that decision-making is transferred from central boards to local hospitals.

The hope is that this will bring down waiting lists and already we see improvements in most areas including Southend.

Law and Order

TO DEAL WITH the increase in crime, spending on law and order has increased more than in any other area—up by eighty-seven per cent in real terms.

The number of police officers has risen by 16,000.

And we have recruited an extra 12,000 civilians to do the desk work for the police with the result that more than 5,400 police officers have been freed to go on the beat.

Those who criticise our campaign on crime should remember that when Labour was in power 5,000 officers left the service. The police in 1979 (the last year of Labour government) were 8,000 under strength and there was even talk of a police strike !

1992, April

Teddy Taylor in one of his rare moments at home when he is not on constituency business

The pensioners

IN EVERY YEAR the retirement pension has been increased to fully reflect the increased living costs.

We have also tried to do more for those who do not have other income.

For example, the Budget changes, along with the April pension increases, mean that the less well off pensioner has been provided with extra amounts ranging from £5.75 to £10.75 a week.

Retirement leaseholders

WE HAVE numerous residential leaseholders in blocks of flats in Southend.

After a great battle, in which Sir Teddy has co-operated with the Retirement Leaseholders' Federation, based in Homecove House, the Government has now committed itself to bringing in Commonhold legislation to give every such leaseholder the right to buy the freehold of their properties at the market rate.

Special congratulations to Mr. Joe Gordon and Mr. Jim Keith, who led a great national campaign from Southend, and who, after a battle, persuaded the Government to act !

"A man's a man for a' that" . . . Teddy at the Lockhart Centre where he gave a recital of Robbie Burns' poetry.

1992, April

208

A Message from your Candidate

Dear Elector,

My family and I have enjoyed twelve happy years living in Southend-on-Sea, and I have always endeavoured to work hard for all the residents, irrespective of how they vote.

I have always regarded my first task as being the duty to serve the community and to make myself available to my constituents. My second duty is to fight for Southend in Parliament.

We have had a few victories for Southend since the last election.

For example, the unfair Government grant system, which gave Southend less than others, has been changed. The £69 extra per head last year on top of the £130 council grant, has placed us on a fair and equal footing.

Likewise, over health spending — the new weighted capitation system will bring at least an extra £10m. to Southend health care and hospitals.

On the Fenchurch Street line progress has still to come, but at least B.R. and the Government have now committed themselves to a £260m. programme to refurbish the signalling and the rolling stock. However, I will keep on pressing, along with the active rail travellers' groups, until it actually happens.

On the economy, it would be dishonest not to admit freely that the curse of unemployment and business misery is serious and worrying. It would also be dishonest not to admit that there are limits on what any government can do to resolve things quickly, partly because of the world recession and partly because of the restrictions placed on interest rate cuts by the Exchange Rate Mechanism of the European Community.

Voters will know that I have always opposed the artificial exchange rate of E.R.M. and voted against it. However, my views are a minority opinion and with all the parties officially committed to the system, the choice facing voters is how we can best escape the current recession.

I believe that there can be little doubt tha the Conservative policy of seeking to control publi spending and trying to reduce taxation is a better answer than the Labour theme of increasing public spending and raising taxes.

If we follow the Labour course the pound will come under pressure, and interest rate cuts—so urgently required—will simply not happen.

The second choice is whether you, the voters, consider that John Major or Neil Kinnock can best lead the country through the difficult problems and decisions which face us.

However, irrespective of the choice made by the electorate generally, if I am re-elected as M.P. for Southend East I shall do everything in my power to serve you all—and to vote in Parliament for what I believe to be in your best interests.

Yours sincerely,

Teddy Taylor

TEDDY'S RECORD...

- [ ] HE LIVES IN SOUTHEND WITH HIS WIFE AND FAMILY—THE LOCAL MAN
- [ ] HE HOLDS A SURGERY FOR CONSTITUENTS EVERY WEEK AND HIS NUMBER IS IN THE PHONE BOOK
- [ ] HE ANSWERS THOUSANDS OF LETTERS EVERY YEAR AND FIGHTS HARD FOR ALL CONSTITUENTS
- [ ] HE IS A REGULAR VISITOR TO THE CLUBS, CHURCH ORGANISATIONS, SCHOOLS, FACTORIES AND EVERYWHERE HE CAN MEET THE PEOPLE
- [ ] HE FIGHTS VIGOROUSLY IN PARLIAMENT FOR SOUTHEND
- [ ] HE REGULARLY TAKES PARTIES OF SCHOOLCHILDREN, PENSIONERS AND RESIDENTS ROUND THE HOUSE OF COMMONS TO LET THEM SEE OUR DEMOCRATIC PARLIAMENT AND HOW IT OPERATES
- [ ] HE FIGHTS FOR WHAT HE BELIEVES IS RIGHT—IRRESPECTIVE OF THE VIEWS OF THE PARTY WHIPS—A MAN OF INDEPENDENT MIND

POLLING DAY: THURSDAY APRIL 9th 1992 — 7 a.m.-10 p.m.

Published by E. W. J. Lockhart, 1 Strand House, 742 Southchurch Road, Southend   Goodyear Printers, 70 Southchurch Avenue, Southend

1992, April

CONSERVATIVE PARTY

SPOTLIGHT on your

CONSERVATIVE

CANDIDATE for POLLING DAY

THURSDAY **11** JUNE

TEDDY TAYLOR

All photographs by courtesy of "Evening Echo"

the man who gets things done!

A WINNER FOR SOUTHEND EAST

TIME TO GET TOUGH ON CRIME

CONSERVATIVE prospective Parliamentary candidate for Southend East Mr. Teddy Taylor has urged magistrates and judges to get tough with offenders convicted of serious crime.

And he has also urged his colleagues standing at the next election to fight to ensure that stronger deterrents are made available particularly for crimes involving violence.

Mr. Taylor told his local Conservative Association that while police numbers had been increased, and more resources put into law and order, the greatest need was to have stronger penalties to strike fear into the hearts of potential criminals.

Callous

Mr. Taylor also urged that special penalties should be available for those who attacked the elderly and the disabled.

"We should have no sympathy with such callous thugs," he insisted.

Mr. Taylor stated that he would again be voting for the return of capital punishment.

He said there was clear evidence that since hanging had been abolished the use of guns by criminals had soared.

Working for charities

SOUTHEND has a great reputation for generosity and the local Conservative prospective Parliamentary candidate for Southend East, Mr. Teddy Taylor, is always willing to help with his presence at fund-raising ventures.

He is pictured right with some local college students who arranged to "kidnap" him as a fund-raising stunt.

Teddy's wife Sheila has also organised events to raise substantial funds for children's charities including the N.S.P.C.C.

The latest was a dinner dance at Shoebury Garrison for the Malcolm Sargent Children's Cancer Fund.

HEALTH SERVICE PROGRESS

FURTHER PROGRESS has been made in reducing the underfunding of the Southend Health Authority, according to Coun. Ernie Lockhart, who is a member of the authority.

And he paid tribute to the strong representations made during the term of the last Conservative Government by Teddy Taylor, M.P. for Southend East, and other local M.P.s in pressing Southend's case with ministers and the Regional Health Authority.

The underfunding had hit Southend hard and at one stage had reached several million pounds.

But since the authority and local M.P.s had initiated a campaign this had been steadily reducing.

Cancer Unit – the battle continues

AN ALL-PARTY CAMPAIGN to save the Southend radiotherapy unit was spearheaded by local Members of Parliament during the last session before the House was dissolved prior to the run-up to the General Election.

After presenting a massive petition to Downing Street along with M.P.s and councillors from the three main parties, Teddy Taylor said: "Although the final decision will not be made until the end of the year by the Secretary of State for Health, the battle must continue strongly until then.

"We must remember that quite apart from the dreadful hardship which the move would mean for Southend patients, the proposal by the region would also cost £4m. extra—not very sensible for the regional authority."

PEACE AND PROSPERITY
—a brighter future

THE OUTLOOK for peace and prosperity was brighter than at any time for decades.

This was the claim made recently by prospective Conservative Parliamentary candidate for Southend East Mr. Teddy Taylor.

"The Tory policy of backing N.A.T.O. 100 per cent, of maintaining our nuclear weapons until arms cuts can be agreed, and of matching Soviet power has kept the peace and now seems more likely to bring about a major arms cut deal," said Mr. Taylor.

"If we had followed the path of nuclear disarmament supported by the Left, the Soviets would have had no incentive to come to the negotiating table."

Mr. Taylor also argued that the outlook for the economy was getting brighter every day.

Outlook brighter

"We've been through a tough time," he said, "but now every indicator is showing an improvement.

"Unemployment is falling every month, interest rates are down again, exports are soaring and taxes are being cut.

"It all adds up to a brighter future."

Family man

TEDDY TAYLOR is a family man.

His home is in Southend at 12 Lynton Road, where he resides with his wife, Sheila, and children John (15), George (12) and Louise, all of whom attend local schools.

M.P.'s RECORD POINTS THE WAY

ALL ELECTIONS are about policies—and this one is no different.

Voters will be working out in their minds which party's policies are most likely to maintain the peace and ensure prosperity.

But elections are also about people; about the men and women who are given the responsibility of representing us in Parliament.

Teddy Taylor's record is clear.

He has gained a reputation for getting things done.

He has provided a splendid service to countless constituents who have sought his help.

He has been a sturdy champion of Southend's interests in Parliament.

And he has shown a healthy independence—speaking out for what he believes in even when in conflict with his own party.

Southend East has been lucky to have such a fine representative.

And it is up to us to support him now for all he has done for us during his time in Parliament.

SCHOOLS MINISTER VISITS SHOEBURY

ANOTHER minister has recently visited the Southend East area where he paid particular interest to education in the constituency.

This time it was Education minister Bob Dunn who visited the Hinguar Street Junior School in Shoeburyness.

Demonstration

During his visit the Minister, who was accompanied by Teddy Taylor, was given a demonstration of computer equipment donated by a local firm to mark the school's centenary.

"I welcome ministerial visits to the constituency," said Mr. Taylor.

"Not only have we a lot to be proud of in Southend, but it gives the leaders of our party the opportunity of getting to know the area."

R.A.F. group brings up Teddy's ton

WHEN fifty-three members of Southend R.A.F. Association paid a visit to the Houses of Parliament as guests of Teddy Taylor it was one which bore a special significance.

For it marked the one hundredth tour undertaken by Mr. Taylor since he was first elected to the House.

3,500 visitors

In all he has shown round about three thousand five hundred visitors.

Parties have included groups of pensioners, schoolchildren, churches and the disabled.

"It is always a pleasure to let constituents see where it all happens at Westminster," he said.

"It also gives voters a chance to understand a little of what goes on in our seat of government.

"After all, Parliament belongs to the people and not to the M.P.s," he concluded.

LOCAL FIRM'S PROGRESS MARKED BY A CHAMPAGNE RECEPTION

BEFORE Parliament was dissolved Teddy Taylor had a very pleasant duty to perform.

He presented a local firm with a bottle of House of Commons champagne to mark a major achievement in expansion and development.

Welcoming the firm's progress, Mr. Taylor said: "Keeping jobs available for the people depends on attracting new firms; on encouraging existing firms to invest and modernise."

Golden year for Taylor clan

THIS is a special year for the Taylor clan.

Sheila Taylor's parents, Mr. and Mrs. Alec Duncan, who live in Wimborne Road, are celebrating their golden wedding.

20

The threat to our democracy

While there are few who would question the fact that MPs, if committed and enthusiastic, can help people to overcome unfairness and injustice, I think that there is far less confidence that MPs can play a meaningful role in changing government policies and the policies of political parties. In fairness, the issue has become more academic with so much power having been transferred to the European Union, where decisions are made in most cases by the majority vote of Ministers from member states and when the European Commission and the European Court can frequently introduce new policies and decisions on the basis of treaties previously approved by member states.

But is this not simply a transfer of power from national Parliaments to the great European Parliament in Strasbourg? Sadly this democratic transfer has never taken place and although it can be argued that the Euro Parliament has some basic powers, in practice it is pretty useless and I genuinely believe that if it were to close its doors tomorrow and cease to exist that few would notice apart from the taxi-drivers of Strasbourg.

But within the remit of the powers still remaining with national Parliaments, do the MPs have effective power and does this power achieve significant change?

I think that there is little doubt that the power still remains and effective MPs can achieve a great deal first in securing information on the basis of constant and repeated written or oral questions and secondly using their votes on key issues.

But how free are MPs to make such decisions?

The answer is, of course, that it is never easy to vote against the Party Whips' advice and the outcome of individual rebellion can range from the loss of Party goodwill to deselection as the party representative in the constituency. A great deal, of course, depends on the party's assessment of the motives for the rebellion. Is it an issue on which the MP feels sincere views or is it perhaps simply a means of causing embarrassment to the party as a form of revenge? The response can vary enormously.

I can well recall that when I was a junior Minister in the Heath Government, having responsibility for health and education in Scotland, I had to face the horrible dilemma stemming from the Prime Minister's decision to seek to join the EU and to sign the Treaty of Rome. It really was a nightmare for me because deep down and on the basis of reading the official documents, I was in no doubt that we would be obliged to surrender a major part of our democracy, that we would be joining up economically with an area in structural decline and that we would be throwing away a huge centre of goodwill and co-operation with the Commonwealth nations which had huge trading potential. Basically I feared that we would move from being a potentially strong world power, committed to democracy, to become a minor player in Western Europe.

The problem for me was that to go against the party would require me to throw away what could have been a substantial political career. It was pointed out to me time and time again that Europe was entering a time of prosperity and growth, that Britain could be left out of a great opportunity if we said no, and that no power would be surrendered to the EU unless our Parliament agreed. Perhaps even more worrying was the fact that the vast majority of the pro-Europe people seemed to be genuinely sincere and not just following the party line.

In fairness, I have to say, the Prime Minister Ted Heath could not have been more helpful or kind in his attitude. I was asked to join him for afternoon tea in the garden of 10 Downing Street and we had quite a chat. He did not seek in any way to question my arguments but put forward instead the basic sentiment that when so many people with ability and experience were for the EU, was it not a mistake for me to throw away an important government office on the basis of opinions which tended to be supported by the old guard and the more traditional Conservatives. Was there not a great opportunity from which we could all benefit?

But when I explained that I thought the decision to join was such a mistake that I just could not live with the consequences of voting for it, Ted simply wished me well and said that he was sorry that I would be leaving his Government.

Ted kept in touch with me after my resignation and actually arranged for me to rejoin the Government in 1974 just before the election which he was to lose. We have often talked about the Euro decision since then and although our views never changed, I will never forget his willingness to come and speak for me at one of the elections in Southend.

Of course I had problems in my Glasgow constituency when I voted against the Third Reading of the Treaty of Rome, but I had no problems whatsoever with the Party Whips who seem to have been given advice to leave me alone with my problems. Of course decisions to vote against one's party on a three line whip are never easy, but quite frankly there is little point in being in Parliament at all if one is going to vote for something which one considers to be wholly wrong for the nation and largely irreversible.

But voting against the party is usually much more cruel and nasty than the pleasant time I had with Ted Heath. The problem with the European Union was that it simply wouldn't go away. There were new treaties every five years or so and some additional constitutional issues of principle which had to be dealt with. Of course it was possible, as some argued, that once the basic decision on membership had been made, the best way forward was to take a positive role to the EU and sit round a table with the other member states seeking improvements. Certainly the structure of the anti-EU group changed rather dramatically in the Conservative Party. Those who opposed the first basic treaty tended to be the more elderly, decent, respectable and perhaps old-fashioned chaps. They felt that something rather improper was happening and that the Conservatives of all people should be cautious.

However, after the passage of the First Treaty, this group tended to disappear and a new group of younger, vigorous and committed MPs came together and they spent a great deal of time, unlike the original rebels, asking questions about the EU. How much money was the Government paying into Brussels and how did this compare with estimates. What had actually happened to our trade with Europe and had it improved as had been suggested on membership day. How was the CAP managing to reform itself, and how was Europe managing to control graft and corruption? The group was made up of around 20 MPs and it was tending to grow in size. However, as usually happens, when the great battle came along over the provision of extra funding for the EU, quite a few of the rebels faded away and we were left with a group known as the Group of Eight, seven of whom voted against the extra cash and one of whom joined the group and committed himself to it.

That group consisted of Christopher Gill, Richard Shepherd, Tony Marlow, John Wilkinson, Teresa Gorman, Sir Richard Body, Nicholas Budgen and myself.

Things were rather different under the Premiership of John Major. Instead of offering us goodwill and expressing regrets, John Major's administration delivered the nastiest blow which it is possible to administer in Parliament, namely the eight MPs had the Whip withdrawn from them. In practice this meant that one simply did not get the Whip's advice notes delivered each week and the eight MPs were denied the right to attend the 1922 Committee and the various party groups at which one can let off steam and make representations to Ministers.

However, the real "meat" of losing the Whip is that constituency parties are given the opportunity or perhaps even the invitation to choose another candidate. Certainly the Group of Eight were well aware of the seriousness of the problems which faced them and I certainly gained the impression that most of them considered that their time had come as a Conservative MP.

However, rather than securing an apologetic response, the Major campaign simply appeared to further enliven the rebels; they started publishing papers on the Euro issue and attracted a great deal of attention as they met once a week to decide how the group should vote.

Thorpe Ward
Polling Day - Thursday 1st May 1997
7 a.m. to 10 p.m.

You will have three voting papers
· one for your Member of Parliament
· one for your County Councillor
· one for your three Southend Councillors

VOTE FOR THE CONSERVATIVE TEAM!

VOTE | **TAYLOR TEDDY** | **X**

for your M.P.

Sir Teddy Taylor has been Southend East Member of Parliament for 16 years and lives with his family in the constituency. He is a caring and thoughtful M.P., well respected and always available to constituents at weekly surgeries locally.

VOTE

AYRE GEOFFREY	**X**
CARR SALLY	**X X**
WHITE DAPHNE	**X X**

as your Thorpe Ward Councillors

AYRE	X
CARR	X
WHITE	X

GEOFFREY AYRE was Mayor of Southend in 1991/92 and is one of the most experienced Southend Councillors. In addition to his Council work Geoffrey is Chairman of Thorpedene Community Centre and of Abbeyfield South East Essex Society.

SALLY CARR has represented Thorpe on Southend Council for 6 years. She is a local school teacher and would bring much needed experience to Southend Council's new education authority.

DAPHNE WHITE is well known throughout the Ward for her energy and efficiency in dealing with the many and varied problems faced by residents. She has served on Southend Council for three years and has taken an active interest in all aspects of the Local Authority.

VOTE | **WHITE DAPHNE** | **X** | County Councillor

Published by Neville Moss, Suite 1, Strand House, 742 Southchurch Road, Southend-on-Sea, Essex SS1 2PS.   Printed by The Rochford Press, Unit 7, Riverside Industrial Estate, South Street, Rochford, Essex SS4 1BL.

ELECTION SPECIAL

SIR TEDDY TAYLOR

the right champion for Rochford and Southend East

It is over sixteen years since Southend East Constituency chose Teddy Taylor to be its Member of Parliament. Elected with only a wafer thin majority of a few hundred votes, he promised to fight for all the people in the Constituency and to battle for the Borough in Parliament. Since then he has served the community so well that he has been re-elected with majorities of over 13,000 - the highest ever recorded for the constituency.

His record is one of impeccable service to the people. A family man with many local interests, he spends much of his time meeting constituents and helping them to solve real problems.

▲ Sir Teddy Taylor in his office

Dedication

But at the same time he has never neglected his duties in the House of Commons, where he fights hard for the interests of the Borough.

The Boundary Commission has now determined that the Constituency should be increased in size to include not only the whole of Southend East but also the Borough of Rochford, the village of Great Wakering, Barling, Sutton and the island of Foulness. Now democracy requires the electors of the new constituency of Rochford and Southend East to select a representative to serve their interests in Westminster.

Sir Teddy Taylor is the right man to fight for us all. He is the right man for the job.

TRUE · TRIED · TRUSTED

About your Candidate

Teddy Taylor lives with his wife and family in Southend. He keeps in touch with his constituents.

Teddy Taylor attends his office in Southchurch Road each week to meet and talk to any constituents who wish to see him, and he works tirelessly to seek to resolve their problems. Last year alone he had more than 1400 interviews with constituents.

Teddy Taylor receives about 10,000 letters each year - he answers them all personally.

Teddy Taylor visits old folks clubs, church organisations, schools and factories throughout the constituency meeting you, the people.

Teddy Taylor speaks up for Southend in Parliament to ensure a fair deal for you and the Borough. He gets results.

Teddy Taylor takes about a thousand residents on tours of Parliament each year - womens groups, pensioners and schoolchildren.

✉ **Postal votes and proxies.** Those who are sick, on holiday or away from home in connection with their work can obtain postal votes or proxy votes. Remember, it is your right to be able to vote, so don't miss this opportunity. Your vote could be vital.

But time is short - so don't delay.
Telephone Teddy Taylor's committee Rooms Southend **600460** *for advice.*

Real progress on the misery line

Sir Teddy has been constantly active in Parliament in demanding action on investment in the Fenchurch Street line which is so vital for the area. When the line was operated by British Rail he campaigned successfully for the new signalling provision which was required. However, with the difficulty of securing new investment with BR, Sir Teddy became a vigorous supporter of the privatisation of the line. At the time, the privatisation idea was opposed by Labour which claimed that the interests of the travelling public would be undermined. Now that privatisation has taken place, the punctuality of the service has improved significantly and we now have a firm pledge that new trains - wholly new trains - will shortly appear on the Fenchurch Street line. Sir Teddy maintains close contact with the management of the privatised firm, to ensure that priority is given to the continuing improvement of this previously poor rail service.

A MAN OF

As Southend Constituents are aware Sir Teddy put his Par
Eight Conservative MPs voted against a plan to provide
confidence vote and then proceeded, with the group, to bl
the Parliamentary Whip which is the equivalent of being
quence of such a loss of the whip is that the M.P. is deprive
selected. However, as the local Conservative Association
port to their M.P., the ban on his Parliamentary membersh
Sir Teddy's courage in standing by his principles over the
Perhaps one of the clearest expressions of support came fr
political affiliations, but which published the following op
*"Sir Teddy Taylor is in the great tradition of independe
subordinate their ambitions and chances of high office to*
*"It is heart-warming to see that there are still a few M.P.s
political careers.*
*"At the end of the day, Britain is not run by Government
personal feelings about Maastricht, one should salute Sir
debate.!"*

▲ Taking part in Essex Walk with Civic leaders

Southend Association of Jewish ex servicemen and women conscecrate a new standard (coinciding with VE/VJ anniversary)
▼

▲ Congratulations for the winners of an in
schools cooking competition

INTEGRITY

...iamentary career wholly at risk when he and the Group of
...substantial additional funding to the European Union in a
...ock the increase in VAT on fuel. For his principles he lost
...expelled from the Parliamentary Party. The usual conse-
...d of the official Party nomination and another candidate is
...i and the community as a whole gave unprecedented sup-
...ip was restored after a long battle.

...years has attracted justifiable praise and support.

...m a local newspaper, the Standard Recorder, which has no
...pinion on their front page in 1993.

...nt backbenchers - men and women of great talent who
...the freedom of speaking forth their convictions.

...like Sir Teddy prepared to put their principles before their

...but by Parliament - 600 individualists. Whatever one's
...Teddy for keeping alive the flame of free thought and open

WHERE DOES TEDDY STAND?

Teddy Taylor is well known for his clear and strong views on
the most important issues affecting the country generally and
his constituents in particular.

Several issues have been raised with the election team during
the campaign and we set out here the standpoint which Teddy
has taken and will continue to take if re-elected to Parliament.

European Union - Sir Teddy has never hidden his opposition to
the transfer of powers to the bureaucracy in Brussels. He resigned
his post as Minister in the Government led by Sir Edward Heath
because of his opposition to the Treaty of Rome. He has voted
against all subsequent treaties. He is wholly opposed to the U.K.'s
participation in economic and monetary union and supports a
referendum on the issue of continued membership of the EU.

VAT Most of the decisions on VAT are now outside the control of
Parliament, a situation which Sir Teddy would like to reverse. He
was one of the rebels whose votes prevented the increase in VAT on
fuel to 17 per cent and, of course, would vote against the extension
of VAT to food or to other items at present zero rated.

THE PIER - Sir Teddy is an enthusiast for the Pier in Southend
and is President of the Pier Society. He supports fully the current
plans to improve the facilities available at the end of the Pier.

THE ELDERLY - Sir Teddy is a champion of the senior citizens
and supports a separate pensioners index of prices to ensure that
pension rises reflect more accurately the needs of the elderly.

GREEN BELT - Sir Teddy supports the preservation of the green
belt which provides necessary breathing space for the Borough of
Southend and ensures the separate identity of the neighbouring
Borough and Villages.

THE GRAMMAR SCHOOLS - Sir Teddy supports the
preservation of the grammar schools in Southend which provide
unique educational opportunities for children from all groups in
society. He believes that the Labour commitment to abolish
selection tests would make the continuance of the grammar schools
virtually impossible.

With his family - at his▲
elder son Lt. John
Taylor's "Wings Parade"

▲ Sir Teddy Taylor at Peter Pan's
Adventure Island, Southend-on-Sea

Joining in the fun at an event at the new
Sports Centre
▼

◄
Digging the first sod of the new Sixth
Form Block at the St. Edmunds Secondary
school in Rochford - an investment which

HEALTH SERVICE FUNDING

Teddy Taylor has fought hard for a better deal on government funding for the hospitals and the health service in the Southend area. Real progress has been made and last year while the average increase in health authority spending was 3.86 per cent, the increase for the South Essex Health Authority, which includes Southend and Rochford, was 7.06 per cent - about the biggest increase in the country. This year, 1997-98 has seen a further improvement with a national increase of 3.93 per cent while the South East Essex increase has been 4.76 per cent. Of course with the ever increasing demands on the health service, cash resources will inevitably be stretched. Sir Teddy will continue to battle for priority for South Essex on the basis that our above average percentage of elderly and retired persons justifies priority in spending from Whitehall.

◄ Celebrating with local scouts

▼ A chat with tea and biscuits at a women's organisation

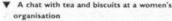

Late into the night but still batting for ▲
Southend in the Commons

THURSDAY 1st MAY 1997
VOTE FOR

| TAYLOR TEDDY | X |

for Rochford & Southend East

Published by N. Moss, Suite One, Strand House, 742 Southchurch Road, Southend on Sea, Essex.
Printed by The Rochford Press, Unit 7, Riverside Ind. Estate, South Street, Rochford Essex SS4 1BL.

ON THE CAMPAIGN TRAIL

SEE AND HEAR TEDDY TAYLOR

SATURDAY, APRIL 12TH
King Edmunds School,
Ashingdon, Rochford

WEDNESDAY, APRIL 16TH
Village Hall
Great Wakering

SATURDAY, APRIL 19TH
St. Bernards School
Milton Road,
Southend-on-Sea

SATURDAY, APRIL 26TH
Shoebury High School
Shoebury

All meetings commence 8 p.m.

ALL WELCOME   YOUR QUESTIONS ANSWERED

"I will deliver common sense solutions to the people of Rochford & Southend East"

Teddy Taylor at Shoebury Model Railway Club

Teddy Taylor with local children at underlines from Nelson school

Teddy and Sheila Taylor attend Ladies Lunch with Michael Howard

Teddy Taylor at Porters Grange Retirement Presentation

Teddy Taylor's five pledges

1. Save the pound and Britain's democracy

2. A tough but fair new policy on asylum seekers

3. Seek a solution to Southend's chronic traffic problems

4. Get a better financial deal for the Rochford Council

5. Fight for a secondary school in Great Wakering

You can telephone Teddy on: 01702 600460

EUROPE

Conservatives consider that too many powers have been transferred to Europe and they are committed to saving the pound and staying out of the Euro. If we surrender our national currency, it would effectively be the end of our independent nation.

BORDER CONTROLS

Conservatives would take a wholly different approach to the asylum seekers issue. Of course, we have a duty to help those who are genuinely being persecuted and whose lives are at risk. But the present policy on asylum seekers is a near shambles. What we need is a policy which will require every applicant to reside in a centre until a decision is made. And we would insist on speedy decisions instead of the present system which can take three years.

THE HEALTH SERVICE

Conservatives have committed themselves to match New Labour's spending on health, but we would work hard to reduce bureaucracy and to reduce waiting lists. This will be a top priority.

EDUCATION

Again we have promised to match Labour's spending, but we believe that the schools will secure more help and more resources with our policy of making all schools "free" so that they can run their own affairs without the cost and delays of bureaucracy.

CRIME

The battle against crime will not succeed unless we have a fully manned police force. Police numbers have fallen by more than 2000 under Labour and the Conservatives will make it a top priority to fill this worrying gap.

LOCAL RATES

The ratepayers have had a really rotten deal with New Labour because the average Band D home has seen a 23% rise in council tax. This is just one of the many stealth tax increases which the Conservatives have committed themselves to stop.

PENSIONS

Conservatives fully accept that the elderly and the disabled have an entitlement to sharing in the increased prosperity of the nation. Nothing is more sickening than New Labour's policy of awarding 75p after elections and a much bigger rise before elections.

On Thursday 7th June 2001, vote

Teddy Taylor
Conservatives X

Teddy Taylor deserves your vote because he fights hard for everyone who needs help, makes himself available and works with everyone in the best interests of the community.

Promoted by Tony Shiffman, Suite 1, Brand House, 742 Southchurch Road, Southend-on-Sea, Essex SS1 2PS on behalf of Teddy Taylor, Suite 1, Brand House, 742 Southchurch Road, Southend-on-Sea, Essex SS1 2PS Printed by Mistral Printers Ltd, 37 Victoria Road, Romford, Essex RM1 2LH

Vote Teddy Taylor
Conservatives

"It's been a real privilege for me to represent Southend and Shoeburyness in Parliament and, since the last election, to serve Barling, Foulness, Great Wakering and Rochford as well.

Teddy Taylor presents electric wheelchair to St Nicholas School

I've tried my best to fight for the area in Parliament and to ensure that it gets a fair share of the resources provided by government. We've achieved quite a few victories for Southend by working together and more recently I've been fighting hard to redress some of the grievances of the areas added to the constituency, the most obvious being the dreadful financial deal which the Rochford Council has had for so many years.

On the party political front, I've never hidden my deep dislike for the media tactics of New Labour which seeks to mislead by pretending that progress has been made when it hasn't been. I also deplore New Labour's policy on the EU and its failure to cope with the serious problem of asylum seekers.

If you re-elect me, I can promise to fight for everyone in the constituency, and to work hard for the community as a whole."

All photographs by kind permission of Southend Times

224

Teddy Taylor's **five pledges**

1. Save the pound and Britain's democracy

2. A tough but fair new policy on asylum seekers

3. Seek a solution to Southend's chronic traffic problems

4. Get a better financial deal for the Rochford Council

5. Fight for a secondary school in Great Wakering

You can telephone Teddy on: 01702 600460

What should you expect from the Conservatives in the next Parliament?

Better public services. We won't just spend more, we'll spend it better. That means we'll make sure the money gets direct to our hospitals and schools rather than being wasted on form filling and bureaucracy.

Lower taxes. Because we have identified £8billion of unnecessary government spending, we'll be able to abolish taxes on savings, cut taxes on pensioners, lower petrol tax and impose less tax on families. Unlike Labour, we won't cancel these out with stealth taxes either.

A war on crime. We're going to put more police on the streets, have tougher sentences and end Labour's crazy policy of releasing prisoners early.

A strong, stable economy. There will be less regulation and less tax on business so that we can have more jobs and prosperity.

A free and independent Britain. Like most people, Conservatives want to be in Europe, not run by Europe. We will keep the Pound.

William Hague

Teddy Taylor

225

TEDDY TAYLOR

the man for you

TRUE TRIED TRUSTED

TEDDY TAYLOR
working for
Rochford and Southend East

Sir Teddy Taylor has been the Member of Parliament for Southend East since 1980 and for Rochford and Southend East since the last election. He lives in the Constituency and has gained the reputation of being a caring and conscientious M.P. He holds weekly surgeries and has seen over 16,000 residents since he was elected M.P. for the area. He receives a very large mail of around 2000 letters per month and answers each one personally. He is always available to constituents and his number is in the phone book.

While never hiding his Conservative party links, he has worked with representatives of all the political parties in the interests of Rochford and Southend East. He is constantly in touch with government Ministers and he gets results. His constituency was the only one in Essex to secure Objective 2 funding which should bring about £15 millions of investment over the next three years.

Jobs, health, schools and the containment of crime are amongst Sir Teddy's top priorities and he also champions the interest of the elderly.

In Parliament he is well respected and is always willing to speak and vote according to his conscience on local and national issues.

CONSERVATIVE.

TEDDY TAYLOR

Sir Teddy Taylor lives in the constituency with his family. His home number is in the telephone directory. He holds a weekly surgery and is always glad to visit local organisations and events. He is always willing to fight hard for constituents and for the local community.

a personal message

❝ It's been a very real privilege to serve Rochford and Southend East and its residents; and I'm now seeking your support and vote to enable me to continue my service for the community ❞

CONSERVATIVE.

Promoted by Tony Smithson on behalf of Teddy Taylor. Both of Suite 1 Strand House 742 Southchurch Road Southend-on-Sea Essex SS1 2PS. Printed by Circle Services (Southend) Ltd. 7 Stock Road Southend-on-Sea Essex SS2 5QN

TEDDY TAYLOR

4 vital things to remember...

■ It's no secret that Sir Teddy has always opposed and voted against EU membership and has on occasions been in conflict with his own Party. However, in this election the parties offer a clear choice. Labour is committed to seeking to join the Euro in the next Parliament and the Conservatives are committed to saving the pound. We're near the end of the road on Euro integration. It's something that really matters for the future of our nation and its freedom.

■ The asylum seekers issue has to be faced up to. Of course we must give help and support to those persecuted in their own countries, but we must speed up the process of decision making and return to their own countries those seeking to enter our country illegally. The failure to take this issue seriously has undermined race relations. Only the Conservatives are committed to a policy of reception centres for asylum seekers and to speedy decisions on their claims.

■ We've seen very substantial rises in tax under Labour. Leading accountants have stated that Labour's spending plans will mean further tax rises. And tax rises nowadays often means adding to the cost of goods and services which hit the poorest hardest of all.

■ There are many issues in our area which demand government action. Underfunding of Rochford Council. Shortage of secondary school places. Traffic congestion in Southend. And many more. The best person to take on these battles is Sir Teddy who has a record for getting things done.

CONSERVATIVE.

Promoted by Tony Smithson on behalf of Teddy Taylor. Both of Suite 1 Strand House 742 Southchurch Road Southend-on-Sea Essex SS1 2PS. Printed by Circle Services (Southend) Ltd. 7 Stock Road Southend-on-Sea Essex SS2 5QN

Taylor: 'Save Our Pound'

Teddy Taylor : Porters Grange School Presentations

Teddy Taylor presents the trophies

Teddy Taylor with Prefect on first official duty

It's no secret that Teddy Taylor is a long standing opponent of EU membership. He's voted against all the Treaties and actually resigned a ministerial post because of his opposition to the Treaty of Rome.

The Single Currency, he argues, is the end of the road in Britain's absorption into a single European state without democracy. He and the Conservative Party are committed to fighting the proposal to join the Euro throughout the next Parliament.

"We've a difficult enough time having an economic policy suitable to all the United Kingdom - how on earth could we have a policy suiting the whole of Europe?

And don't forget that it won't do any good to join up with a group of nations with higher unemployment and higher overall taxation."

Why we need a tough but fair policy for asylum seekers

If the Conservatives are returned to power there will be a fundamental change in policy on asylum seekers.

The present arrangements whereby a multitude of appeals can go on for three years or more and when so many unsuccessful applicants can get lost in the system, will have to be changed. All asylum seekers should remain in central areas until a speedy decision is made. If unsuccessful they must be returned to their homeland immediately. If successful we must go out of our way to make provision for them in our community.

All photographs by kind permission of Southend Times

On Polling Day, your vote will make the difference. If you would like to contact Teddy for any reason, please contact him on:

Vote
Teddy
Taylor
Conservative X

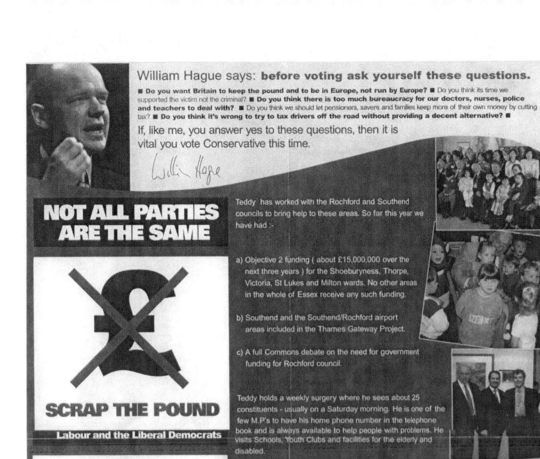

William Hague says: **before voting ask yourself these questions.**

■ **Do you want Britain to keep the pound and to be in Europe, not run by Europe?** ■ Do you think its time we supported the victim not the criminal? ■ **Do you think there is too much bureaucracy for our doctors, nurses, police and teachers to deal with?** ■ Do you think we should let pensioners, savers and families keep more of their own money by cutting tax? ■ **Do you think it's wrong to try to tax drivers off the road without providing a decent alternative?** ■

If, like me, you answer yes to these questions, then it is vital you vote Conservative this time.

William Hague

NOT ALL PARTIES ARE THE SAME

SCRAP THE POUND

Labour and the Liberal Democrats

SAVE THE POUND

Vote for common sense.
Vote Conservatives X

Teddy has worked with the Rochford and Southend councils to bring help to these areas. So far this year we have had :-

a) Objective 2 funding (about £15,000,000 over the next three years) for the Shoeburyness, Thorpe, Victoria, St Lukes and Milton wards. No other areas in the whole of Essex receive any such funding.

b) Southend and the Southend/Rochford airport areas included in the Thames Gateway Project.

c) A full Commons debate on the need for government funding for Rochford council.

Teddy holds a weekly surgery where he sees about 25 constituents - usually on a Saturday morning. He is one of the few M.P's to have his home phone number in the telephone book and is always available to help people with problems. He visits Schools, Youth Clubs and facilities for the elderly and disabled.

With other seaside M.P's, he has persuaded the Conservative leadership that seaside towns have special needs and problems which require special help. The result is the seaside manifesto which commits a future Conservative Government to give considerable extra funding and facilities to seaside towns.

It's no secret that Teddy has had differences of opinion with his party on some issues. In the recent vote on fox hunting he was one of a handful voting against hunting with hounds. But he always tells his constituents his opinions and sticks to them.

On Thursday 7th June 2001, vote
Teddy
Taylor

You can telephone Teddy on: 01702 600460

Conservatives
www.conservatives.com

Common Sense

From Teddy Taylor
Conservative Candidate for Rochford & Southend East

General Election
Special Edition

Teddy Taylor - fighting for the whole community

Since he was elected to represent our area, Teddy has made public service his aim. He lives in the constituency and his home and office phone numbers are in the phone book. He also holds a weekly surgery - usually on a Saturday morning - when he normally sees about 20 to 25 constituents.

He has always fought like a tiger in Parliament for Southend, and now he has embarked on a crusade in Parliament to get a better financial deal for Rochford which he believes has been unfairly dealt with by governments of both parties in recent years. The latest advances in Southend are the Borough's admission to the Thames Gateway project and

Teddy Taylor at Pre-school group

an astonishing granting of Objective 2 grants to all of Southend East except Southchurch - which is estimated to involve £15,000,000 over the next three years.
He is never afraid to speak up

for what he believes in and is now pressing for a tough but fair policy on asylum seekers. He believes that if the rules are not tightened, the good community relations which Southend has always enjoyed will be undermined.

Teddy Taylor's five pledges:

1. Save the pound and Britain's democracy

2. A tough but fair new policy on asylum seekers

3. Seek a solution to Southend's chronic traffic problems

4. Get a better financial deal for the Rochford Council

5. Fight for a secondary school in Great Wakering

A message from William Hague

At this General Election, you can decide what kind of country you want to live in.

How safe is our country?
Conservatives will wage war on the criminal. Labour have cut police numbers and violent crime is rising. I will put more police back in our communities and ensure they spend their time policing not bogged down in paperwork.

Spending your money wisely.
Our hard working teachers and

nurses deserve to be allowed to do their jobs. Conservatives will spend your money better, cut your taxes.

Europe and keep our pound. I offer a very straightforward policy. Britain should be in Europe not run by Europe and we will keep the Pound. Labour want to scrap the Pound which will cost nearly £1,000 for every voter.

Conservatives Common Sense policies can win this election.

Published by Tony Smithson, Suite 1, Strand House, 742 Southchurch Road, Southend on Sea SS1 2PS
Printed by Metloc Printers Limited, 37 Victoria Road, Romford, Essex RM1 2LH

www.conservatives.com

Perhaps the greatest achievement of the Group of Eight was to keep the anti-market sentiment alive, to circulate the facts, figures and arguments and to encourage the many anti-marketeers in the constituency parties to stay alive politically and to join in the crusade. Certainly, when the Maastrict Bill – one of the many Treaties, came upon us, the anti-market group became a huge and effective Parliamentary body. The argument had become a respectable one and some of the giants like Iain Duncan Smith became involved.

But what did we achieve with the Euro rebellions? For a start we kept the issue alive and helped to get many of the opinion-formers and magazines to put across the anti-market case as a respectable argument. It cheered us all up immensely to see the massive change of opinion within industry and commerce. The British industrialists had previously been almost unanimous in supporting the EU but the massive bureaucracy costs and problems stemming from the EU have certainly brought about a real change.

Even the Conservative Party, although rather reluctant to talk about the issue at all because of the divisions which this produces, has become astonishingly eurosceptic. It was agreeable to see the commitment in the 2005 manifesto indicating that a Conservative Government would withdraw Britain from the Common Fisheries Policy.

Of course the Conservatives didn't quite win this election, although they did much better. So we will just have to wait until the next election to see how such a policy would be implemented. In fairness, as the opponents have pointed out so often, membership of the EU is not like normal Bills in Parliament which can be approved and then cancelled – with Europe we actually have to hand power over in a situation which has been described as irreversible and irrevocable. We should also remember that the only nation which ever escaped from the EU is Greenland, which achieved this only when every member state passed laws to allow the exclusion of this huge island. In preparing for the future, it is vital that we should work out the real power which member states still have in Europe, and use this as a means of creating a more meaningful arrangement in the EU. If possible there should be an exit clause. Strange to say, although I was quite horrified by the implications of the European Constitution, which fell by the wayside after the glorious referenda in Holland and France, we should not forget that this Constitution for the first time made provision for withdrawal. In fairness, it was a lengthy process, with a procedure for negotiations over a two year period. However, if these long negotiations did not achieve anything, the Treaty provided for the member state to withdraw.

Europe has been only one of a few causes which I have pursued during my 41 years membership of the House of Commons. My first rebellion was over the policy so many years ago over what was then called Rhodesia and which is now Zimbabwe. I gained the impression during a visit to Angola, Mozambique and Rhodesia that none of these countries would do well with self government and I gained the impression that Iain Smith had a great deal of genuine support amongst the African majority. Of course my views were very much minority ones, but it is tragic to see what has happened since to these potentially great and wealthy nations.

I have never been an enthusiast for Scottish devolution and I also caused some problems by seeking to put forward arguments on behalf of

Libya and Iran, although I have no financial or other interest in these nations.

What really upset me on Middle East policy was what appeared to me to be the hypocrisy of the West.

I was one of the rebels on the Iraqi war vote in the Commons, although I was sad to disagree with Iain Duncan Smith, who is certainly one of the most trustworthy and straight politicians I have ever seen in the House. Certainly, I received a large number of abusive letters for the stance I took, but in fairness, public opinion seems to have changed a great deal in the interim. I believe that the vital message we should seek to take from the Middle East crisis, is that the best way forward is to seek to let the people of these nations seek to resolve their own problems. It will not be all that easy because many of the nations have artificial frontiers fixed by the West many years ago.

*Being assaulted by the Chairman of Rochford Council, raising
funds for charity*

21

Working in the constituency

Southend-on-Sea has been astonishingly kind to me as a difficult and rather rebellious member of the Conservative party and I will never forget the total support they gave me when I was for a while expelled from the Parliamentary Party during John Major's period in office.

This support at the time rather reminded me of the advice I had from an old Southendian when I arrived in the borough. "You will find that they are not like the nasty Scots who always want to fight each other – if you do your job well here they will support you whether you are a Conservative or a communist".

Certainly I do recall that in the great battles that followed we had in the Conservative party in Scotland, over matters like the EU, devolution and agriculture, the people who disagreed with me within the Conservative Party gave the impression that my public hanging would be justified while those who agreed with me seemed to be more enthusiastic about swings against the Tories in constituencies represented by "the softies" than if there was a collapse of a Labour vote.

By comparison in Southend, the great majority of the people did not seem to be terribly interested in politics at all and they gave support if, and only if, they regarded you as a champion of the constituency in Westminster and a good adviser to local people with problems.

Of course there was also the negative side. If a march was being organised to deplore the waste in the EU, we had no difficulty filling up a bus of protestors from Glasgow, but it wasn't so easy to motivate protestors in Southend.

But what about the borough itself?

The most significant aspect of the town is that most of the buildings date back no further than 1850. Benjamin Disraeli, who had a rather clever way of putting forward arguments in a few words, described Southend in 1833 as " a row of houses called a town". Some twenty years later, a comprehensive study produced in Chambers Journal described it as "one long strip of houses, a strange jumble of old mansions, cottages, shops, tarry boathouses and boat building sheds, fishermens' dwellings hung over with nets and public houses". It certainly doesn't sound too exciting. In fairness, there are quite a few old buildings in the Borough and quite a bit of evidence in various sites of Roman and Saxon activity.

What revolutionised the area was the introduction of trains to and from London in 1888, the service from Southend to Fenchurch Street in London was initiated and the following year a second line was opened which linked Southend to Liverpool Street. At the same time the Southend pier, which had existed from about 1829, was rebuilt and modernised with rail transport; and being the longest leisure pier in the world by far at over a mile and a third, the scope for expansion was unprecedented. The pier still remains although in fairness we have had major problems with fires on several occasions.

The borough of Southend includes Shoeburyness on the east side and Leigh on Sea on the west side. It used to be two constituencies with a line right down the middle of the town, but the alleged reduction in the size of the population, although house numbers have increased, has resulted in the Southend East constituency being expanded to include Great Wakering, a delightful and rather ancient village, Rochford - which has been an active market town since the days before King Henry the Eighth - and Barling, which is a historic and upmarket area with much agriculture. This constituency expansion created some problems because Southend and Rochford always seem to have been in conflict, perhaps because Southend was in favour of development and expansion and Rochford was in favour of retaining its history and opposing change.

I first became aware of the Rochford/Southend problem many years ago at Glasgow University when we were advised in our studies of the significance of the "Peculiar People" which was a church established in old Rochford. It was all started up by a James Banyard who was born in 1800 and who had a dreadful reputation for drunkenness and many other sins. However, one day after losing all his money at a Fayre in Pagelsham, he decided to reform and to establish a new church called the Peculiar People – a phrase taken from the book of Deuteronomy – and his enthusiasm and commitment, which included a rejection of medical treatment and its replacement by miracles initiated at the new church, resulted in a massive upsurge in Rochford Peculiar People churches. He decided to move in a great march to Southend to start off a similar revival there but when he reached the borough, he was stoned by local residents, who told him in loud voices that if it were sinners he was looking for he would be better to return to Rochford where sin was endemic!

This traditional hostility didn't help the constituency transformation and to make matters worse, the new area had nothing but Labour and

Liberal councillors with the exception of one Conservative, Roy Pearson, in Great Wakering and one Independent councillor in Barling.

However, eventually everything went well and a new understanding was developed between the two areas. At the same time there was a near revolution in political attitudes with all councillors in the new area being Conservative with the exception of one delightful lady who is the only Labour councillor representing the old borough of Rochford.

But how have things gone in Southend?

I was certainly delighted that my initial local party chairman, Derek Streeton and his deputy, Frank Paveley, both shared my views on the EU. They were both fully committed party enthusiasts. Both helped me enormously in getting to know and work with the local councillors.

When I arrived in the area, there were two wards, Thorpe Bay and Southchurch, each with three councillors, who returned Conservatives. By comparison, the councillors for Shoeburyness, Victoria and St Lukes were Labour and we had the Milton ward right in the heart of the borough, where it was regarded as marginal, but at the same time, a deteriorating area. However, in the meantime, things have changed. Shoebury, because of its expansion in size, has become two separate wards and they are solid Conservative. The same has happened in Milton and we have even started to win again in St Lukes. There is no doubt that the committed work of the Conservative councillors and their contact with the people has helped enormously. We have never had Liberal councillors in the east side of Southend, although I have to say that the Labour councillors, including those who have faded away, all seemed to be delightful chaps, who were wholly trustworthy. My relations with Labour in the South have been good ever since the by-election where I scraped through and when the Labour candidate, Colin George, who has been a friend ever since, could have won the seat if he had played the campaign dirtily.

But what is special about Southend?

Its economy depends quite a bit on visitors and on sunny days on the sea front, you see an astonishing number of people. In fairness, when I arrived in 1980, I was told that the sea front was dying and that the outlook for the amusement arcades and the pier was grim. However, the disaster has never come through, largely because Philip Miller who runs Adventure Island and other entertainment facilities on the sea front invested a great deal in equipment so that the area is still attractive to visitors.

Other features which are special in Southend include the education arrangements. Although Southend is in no sense an upmarket area as a whole, our education results have always been well above the country average. One of the reasons may be that our education is rather unusual in that we have four grammar schools, two for boys and two for girls in the borough and they can take in over 20% of the school community. These broad based grammar schools are not seen much in other areas of England or Scotland but the practice is the virtual norm in Ulster, where, as in Scotland, the exam results are well above the national average.

Another special feature is that our two secondary Catholic schools St Bernards and St Thomas More are both single sex schools and their extremely good exam results rather prove the point that single sex schools can improve the exam outcome, particularly in the case of boys.

240

Southend also has good communications with London in our rail services, which are about the best in the UK for reliability. Traffic is however still a problem because of congestion and for many years we have been pressing for a ring road. Signs are now more encouraging.

Southend also has its airport. I have done all in my power to secure the retention of the airport because it contributes a great deal to the local economy and to the potential for industry and commerce. Of course there have been quite a few who have opposed its development in every way, but happily, its future now seems to be secure.

Industry and commerce are always a problem for Southend and apart from the Customs and Excise VAT office and the Keymed organisation which provides high quality goods for the Health Service, there are few major employers. One of the biggest problems these days is on the commercial side, where there are many offices to let near the town centre. Health Service provision in Southend is relatively good and there is a large hospital with a good reputation.

But how have politics developed in Southend and why has there been such a movement towards the Conservatives compared with the rest of the country?

Without a doubt, the hard work of local councillors has made a huge difference. We have tried to concentrate on service to the people rather than party bashing. We have never had a qualified agent, but have always had a full-time Party secretary who is available every day to answer questions or to help to make contact with the MP or the councillors.

The quality of councillors cannot be over emphasised.

When I look back at election times when because we did not have a qualified agent, I had to rely on councillors to organise the campaign and likewise councillors have filled the role of Party officials. When I think of Neville Moss, a councillor and former mayor, who acted as my election agent in some of the more difficult times, I genuinely cannot think of anyone who could have done a better job.

Likewise, councillors and former mayors, like Geoffrey Ayre and Tony North did a remarkable job as Party Chairman again in the most difficult times and I could not have found better. Another person who acted twice as my election agent was Tony Smithson, who concentrated on showing that Conservatism should mean good service to the people. I could list a very large number of active and sincere councillors and certainly the advice I would give to the Conservative Party is that if they wish to do well in election campaigns, the strongest foundation is an army of councillors, officials and candidates who will be willing to work hard for the people. That, after all, is what politics is meant to be about.

Another "must" for party success is a speedy and effective response to all constituency enquiries. Nothing turns people away from party politics more than a feeling that issues which they regard as important are not treated seriously by their elected representative. So to all future would-be MPs I would say that the selection of committed, sincere secretaries who are willing to go the extra mile in providing speedy and effective production of replies for the MP is very very important. I was particularly lucky in Southend to have had a whole series of excellent secretaries and in my final years I had superb service from Elizabeth Day, Sue Tuhill and Helen Morgan who together helped me to provide good service to the people of Southend and Rochford.

But has it all been worthwhile?

Above: William Hague, Leader of the Party, at the time visiting Southend, and walking down the High Street
Below: Iain Duncan Smith on a visit to Southend, and my daughter Louise

The Freedom of the Borough document with the Mayor and the
Town Clerk

The local community couldn't be nicer and I seem to have been appointed honorary President of a multitude of organisations and charities. But I have a sinking feeling that this is more related to my endeavours to help people with problems rather than to support the crusades which I championed.

And sadly on the broader front, things aren't looking too good. The standing of politicians seems to have slumped. I'll never forget the day at Westminster in 1964 when I and other M.P.s were going in the front entrance to attend the formal re-opening of Parliament. Nobody knew who we were or which parties we represented. But they clapped as we walked past. In fairness they didn't cheer, but they clearly believed that we were rendering an important service to democracy and to the people (and no doubt sacrificing other opportunities which wise and courageous people could secure if they were less patriotic).

Sadly, this assessment seems to have changed. People are aware that the great institution which used to determine all the taxes and laws has had its power surrendered a great deal to Brussels. And quite apart from this undermining of power, the host of allowances for M.P.s has not helped their standing because they are regarded as an invitation to cheat.

As I write these depressing words, the next election which the voters are facing is the European Parliament vote. And what on earth are we to vote about? The power in Europe, sadly, does not belong to the people, and there is no way in which voter can even offer opinions on issues. We don't even have the right to choose our representatives. Instead we have areas for voting and the parties, on the basis of their percentage vote, determine who from their lists will go to the European Parliament.

So where should we go, and what should we do? This is the nightmare facing the eurosceptics. And the biggest problem of all is that the public, which seem to be more hostile to Europe than ever, have largely switched off and find it difficult to see who they should follow, campaign for and vote for. Of course there are groups arguing for leaving the EU. But the problem is how could they actually secure this. And to be truthful without being too unfair, some have the impression that the vigorous revolutionaries have become quiet shellfish enjoying the Strasbourg lifestyle.

So what is the way forward? The first step must be to ensure that people are told the truth about Europe. How much does it cost us every minute in contributions to the EU? Should we not be worried that the EU is the only major political institution in the world where the auditors have declined to sign the accounts for 13 years?. What is the impact we have on the Third World by our grotesque common agricultural policy which pays our farmers more than world prices but which also provides substantial subsidies for the dumping of surplus production into the rest of the world?

Next we must argue for euro legislation to be altered to establish the structure as a voluntary organisation which nations could leave if their people wanted to. There was such a provision within the Lisbon Treaty and it would be great if this small part of this rather worrying treaty might be revived.

The one simple message, however, which we must never forget and which I have tried hard to promote is that the people must not go to sleep on their democratic opportunities. If I have helped to keep this crusade alive, at least I can seek to reassure myself that it has all been worthwhile.

22

Parting Shots

15th March 2005

Dear Mrs. Taylor

It gives me the greatest pleasure to send my congratulations to Teddy on his forty years in the House of Commons.

I am genuinely sorry that he has decided to retire after only forty years in the House and I can assure him he will be genuinely missed by friend and foe alike.

I well recall the many and varied contactd we had in politics and I am sorry now that he is leaving them at a time when he is probably most needed.

I send him my personal thanks and all my good wishes.

Teo Heath

The Rt Hon Sir Edward Heath KG MBE

May I add my own heartfelt good wishes to the many others which will have been expressed tonight as you pay tribute to Teddy Taylor.

When Teddy first entered the House of Commons after the 1964 General Election he was part of an enthusiastic new intake who could not wait to badger and harry Labour at every opportunity. That enthusiasm for the political battle and determination that we must carry the fight to our enemies is still as strong in Teddy today as it was four decades ago.

As a backbencher Teddy is searching in his questions and probing in his argument. As a minister he was a valiant defender of our policies to turn back the tide of socialism. And as a constituency MP he has been tireless in representing local interests and local people.

In a world where political style and presentation are valued over political principles, Teddy is a refreshing antidote. He does not hold his beliefs lightly but nor, as his many friends will tell you, does he hold them unbendingly. Teddy has always been prepared to listen to those who disagreed with him with courtesy and respect – even if in reply he went on to demolish their arguments!

We could not have achieved all we did in the 1980s if it had not been for the steadfast determination of colleagues like Teddy and I shall be forever grateful for the support he showed to me for all those years.

Teddy, thank you, and have a wonderful evening.

Margaret Thatcher

 March 2005

Teddy is a remarkable figure, whose time in Parliament has covered the full range of fortunes for the Conservative Party from the high points of Government to the low points of Opposition.

I came into Parliament in 1992 to find Teddy at the forefront of the charge against the Maastricht Treaty and I can still remember some of those great speeches of his with all the trade mark devices used to put off those intervening or answering him. In particular I remember in one lengthy speech by Teddy to a fairly full House he was intervened on by another Conservative who did not share his views on Europe. Just as Teddy was giving way, he looked at his watch, tapped it and said "I don't have a lot of time" and sat down. As he began, he raised his wrist, tapped his watch again and muttered that time was short. He repeated this to the amusement of the House. The poor man never stood a chance and his question died on his lips.

Teddy is one of the most honest, straightforward and decent politicians and it has been my privilege to know him. His record on Europe and other critical matters has been matchless and the very fact that the Conservative Party is now essentially a Euro sceptic party owes a huge amount to Teddy's persistence. I know of nobody in the House on any side who has a bad word to say about Teddy. Even when in fundamental disagreement he is universally liked.

I will personally be very sorry to see Teddy go and I also know that his style of politics sadly leaves with him, as the days of the powerful speech and important cross examination are sliding away from the House of Commons to be replaced by inane sound bites.

I wish Teddy and Sheila a good retirement. Sheila of course, as everybody knows, has been wonderfully long suffering in putting up with Teddy's complete dedication to his constituents and his causes (and his cigarettes!). In fact Sheila has been a critical partner in Teddy's remarkable career.

May you both have a more relaxing time away from this hothouse, but I know this much, the House of Commons will be infinitely worse off without you Teddy, here to remind us all of what we could be and perhaps even what we should be.

The Rt Hon Iain Duncan Smith MP

HOUSE OF COMMONS

LONDON SW1A 0AA

LEADER OF THE OPPOSITION

March 2005

Dinner for Sir Teddy Taylor

I am delighted to send a message of support for tonight's event, in honour of Teddy's 25 years as the Member for Southend and his 40 years' distinguished service to the House.

Teddy and I have some things in common. We both first fought seats in the 1960s in areas which are now regarded as Labour strongholds - Teddy in Glasgow and I, two years later, in Liverpool. Teddy had much more success.

Since then he has had a most distinguished career, both north and south of the border. Contrary to popular opinion, some MPs do enter Parliament with an unbending commitment to their principles and beliefs. Indeed, some even end their time with these attributes. But few maintain them for forty years as a minister, shadow minister and back-bencher.

Teddy has done so. Most famously on Europe, but also on causes as diverse as animal welfare and law and order, he has devoted energy and enthusiasm to everything he champions. Even when we haven't seen eye to eye on an issue, the articulate and indefatigable way in which Teddy has put his case has won admirers on all sides.

To those who know Teddy at Westminster, it comes as no surprise that he is renowned also as an assiduous constituency MP in Rochford & Southend East. It is a tribute to him that he will be as badly missed there as he will be in Parliament.

I wish Teddy well. I am sure tonight's event will be most enjoyable – and thoroughly well-deserved.

MICHAEL HOWARD

Mr Speaker

Speaker's House   Westminster   London   SW1A 0AA

19 March 2005

Dear Sir Teddy,

May I convey my heartiest congratulations on your completion of 40 years in the House of Commons.

I will not be the only one who is sad to hear that you will be leaving the House. Members from every party hold you in the highest regard.

In the House of Commons a Member has to win respect, and you have been able to do so by fighting for your constituents, and also tenaciously campaigning for the causes you believe in.

Being a fellow Glaswegian, I can still remember when you were a campaigning councillor in the old Glasgow Corporation, and when you were also Chairman of the Glasgow Central Young Conservatives. Believe it or not, you won the respect of all the members of the Springburn constituency Labour Party. Delegates well remember how you fought a very tough fight in 1959 against the sitting Labour Member of Parliament, John Forman MP. They still recognise the fact that you were the only candidate to secure 10,358 Conservative votes in what was regarded as a Labour stronghold. They did admit that they felt uneasy at the thought that you might return for another battle at the next General Election!

I think that the Springburn Labour Party heaved a sigh of relief when you were adopted for Glasgow Cathcart, a seat which you held against all the odds from 1964 to 1979. To this day many constituents in Cathcart speak of you very fondly indeed.

It was the good fortune of the House, that the people of Southend-on-Sea elected you as their Member of Parliament. I will never forget when I became Speaker, that you were one of the first Members to congratulate me in your typically kind way.

I don't think I've ever told you the story of when Mary and I went to see the famous Riverdance show at the Hammersmith Apollo. Whilst we were waiting in the queue there were many theatregoers coming off of luxury coaches. Mary pointed out that one of the coaches was from Southend-on-Sea and was named Sir Teddy Taylor. I replied that you wouldn't get a bus named after Michael Martin in Springburn!

I wish you, Sheila and all of your lovely family every success for the future. My thoughts will be with you tonight when you are enjoying the hospitality and tributes from all of your friends.

Yours

Speaker

251

Right Honourable LORD TEBBIT CH

House of Lords
LONDON SW1A 0PW

FROM LORD TEBBIT FOR THE DINNER ON SATURDAY 19 MARCH

When I was first elected to the Commons as Member for Epping in 1970, Teddy had already been in the House for six years and made his mark as a hard headed uncompromising Tory.

I learned a lot from watching him in the House. His sharpness and directness were obvious enough, so, too, was his mastery of procedure. Less obvious was the thought which had gone into the preparation of what sometimes looked like even very short speeches.

It is a pity in every way that during Teddy's last years in the Commons there have been massive Labour majorities, for as a parliamentarian Teddy was at his best harrying to the death Jim Callaghan's government during 1978 and 1979.

Teddy was in many, but not all, respects one of the outriders of Thatcherism, especially its appeal to working class voters and later the classless voters of Essex. It was at times just a little bit difficult to know if he was being entirely serious or whether you were being gently set up!

I recollect that when I visited his former constituency of Glasgow Cathcart in the days when the Tories were a powerful force in Scotland, he briefed me very thoroughly.

"Oh, one other thing" he added. "Don't let them know I'm a Conservative or I'll never be re-elected".

I never doubted he was a Conservative – and one whose anti-European Community views were ahead of his time – but more important even, being a Conservative Teddy was and is a patriot.

Westminster will miss him. We need more like him to stem the tide of politically correct Euro socialism which threatens to extinguish this kingdom's independence.

THANK YOU TEDDY.

23

What of the future?

Of course it is one of the failings of most politicians that they regard themselves as the unique source of wisdom, but I have to say that I think there is clear evidence that we are facing some major problems and ignoring some opportunities. There are just a few I would wish to specify.

1. We have a form of government in Britain that has worked well and we should seek to retain it.

The basic principle of our democracy is that people are in charge – they select the MPs and they decide whether a change of Government is required. Our democracy also depends on the relative independence of the MPs who are selected by groups within the constituencies.

The danger to this comes of course, from the EU which has taken much of the power and has created a situation when the views of the people cannot find a way to express themselves. Just as important has been the withering away of the power of the people to select candidates with the power being transferred to their political parties. Many of our Scottish and Welsh MPs are elected indirectly through the proportional representation system and likewise the members of the Euro Parliament are all elected on an area basis with the top candidates being selected by the parties.

The changes are all in the wrong direction and I think it is vital that we should seek to hold on to our constitutional assets.

2. We now have far too many politicians.

When I was first elected to Westminster all the power was there and the responsibility taken seriously.

But now we have Euro MPs Welsh and Scottish MPs and other regional organisations. They cost a great deal of money but perhaps more significantly, the power is fading away from the control of this ever increasing army. The least we should do is to commit ourselves to giving the people of Scotland and Wales, the opportunity to have another referendum to decide if they wish to retain their local parliaments. The impression I have is that most people in both countries are far from enthusiastic about their new parliaments and the least we should do is to give them a chance to decide the issue.

3. I believe that there is a case for reviewing the size of Government and its many institutions.

One of the most frightening figures is to see the massive change in the percentage of the population which is involved in the business of government. Of course there are always new challenges to face up to, but at the same time, we need more urgently than ever a comprehensive review of the size of government and the need to remove much of the bureaucratic empire.

4. We must adopt a fairer and less hypocritical attitude to the rest of the world.

It seems really cruel and heartless for us to express concern about poverty in the third world but at the same time to enforce a ludicrous agricultural policy which pours highly subsidised food into the third world. All we do is to deprive the third world of fair trade and a reasonable return from their investment. The manner in which we have managed sugar in Europe is one of the best examples of unfairness and hypocrisy and we need to adopt a policy of fairness and truthfulness to all nations and it really is ridiculous that so called supporters of democracy devote so much of their endeavours to helping the least democratic nations in the world. Most of all we should accept that we have no right to be the emperors of the world – it is a task we do not perform well.

To give one example, we should look at the detail of our recent contact with Iran. I can recall a few years ago we saw how Iran's attempt to get rid of the Shah of Persia and to introduce a form of democracy took place at a time when the US was supplying Iran with a massive amount of weapons of mass destruction However, when the Shah was removed from power, the US changed its policy and supplied the weapons to Saddam Hussein, who was a dictator running Iraq. Thereafter Saddam Hussein initiated an invasion of Iran, and many hundreds of thousands of lives were lost. The details of the weapons supplied originally to Iran are recorded in the Reigle report of the US senate. What possible justification was there for this episode? - apart from the basic point that the Shah was a friend of America and the elected representatives in Iran were not regarded in the same positive way.

If we endeavour to solve the many problems facing the Middle East my belief is that we would make more progress if we treated the various nations there with dignity and respect.

Another good example of this is my experiences in Libya. I paid a visit there at a time when Mr. Gadaffi appeared to have no friends in the world and when I was advised that it would be dangerous to travel there. However, as so often before, I found that the foreign office assessment of nations was not too accurate. I visited Mr. Gadaffi on my first visit there and several times thereafter. During my first visit he agreed to cancel the provision he had made for the supply of weapons to the IRA and to many other terrorist groups in then world. These massive changes in policy have been maintained.

The main feature for me on my visit to Libya was to see the actual country itself and the services provided to the community. Of course there is always the danger of being misled, but I can only say that as a person who has no financial or other interests in nations like Libya and Iran my assessment was that they had many positive features which sadly are not communicated to our people. My experience in the world is that those countries which the West approves of are often the most horrible nations for people to live in while those they disapprove of are often liberal and exciting nations which people seem happy to live in.

The final point – number five to be precise – I would like to make is the need for all of us to face up to the consequences of progress.

Whenever one observes the massive increase in the number of cars and lorries, one wonders what on earth we will do when the supply of oil fades out. Likewise the huge increase in the use of aeroplanes will have consequences for the environment and the rather surprising alterations in the weather all over the world should persuade us all that we have to think about managing the future. Surely this is an area of activity where the world could work together and perhaps move away from the situation when we invariably seem to be in conflict.

And perhaps the most obvious common factor in all such discussions and reviews is telling people the truth. My limited experience of politics and democracy is that truth is the most effective and helpful weapon and it is one which we should all use more often.

With Colonel Gadaffi

Appendix: From *The Observer,* 18 August 1996

Nutty but nice

Teddy Taylor; the only Bob Marley fan ever
to join the Monday Club

by Andrew Billen

If there is such a thing as the opposite of an autobiographical novel, *Hearts of Stone* is it. Written by Teddy Taylor when he was 31, it relates the misadventures of Gilbey Horn, a Tory backbencher of around Taylor's present years.

The whips' office has a file on Horn: 'Fifty-six years of age, bald, tubby .., majority has steadily decline, showing that the electors are acutely aware of his general uselessness. Intensely loyal and never out of step ... Would back King Kong all the way if he was elected to lead the Party.'

It may be a *roman à clef*, but the *clef* is not Teddy Taylor. In almost every respect save his Scottishness, his hair loss and his age (he is actually 59), Teddy Taylor - Sir Teddy since 1991 -has not become Gilbey Horn.

Horn gets inebriated at a constituency meeting; Taylor has never tasted alcohol. Horn is perennially broke; Taylor has just voted against the MPs' pay rise. Horn is on the brink of deselection; Taylor's local party told Central Office to 'jump off the pier' when it suggested dropping him when he lost the whip in 1994 for voting against the Government over Europe. His constituents in Southend East love him, increasing his majority at every opportunity since grudgingly electing him their MP in a by-election in 1980.

Blind loyalty to party, meanwhile, is not his thing at all. He is the complete rebel with many a cause, and only last week ticked off Central Office for demonising Tony Blair. When Horn wins the private members ballot he hasn't a clue what Bill to sponsor; Taylor, in contrast, maintains a healthy stable of hobby horses — although you wouldn't want to put your money on any of them, since no cause is truly lost until Taylor backs it. His triumphs are small: securing a loan for an Asian constituent who came to one of his weekly surgeries, a change in the law permitting denturists to fit false teeth.

'My problem in life,' he says, 'is that I have always had these obsessions - not obsessions, things I have felt very strongly about — and I can't really relax. My wife, Sheila, often says to me: "Why can't you forget about it for a while?" You see I am utterly — this is probably a problem — I am terribly obsessed about the European Community. I am the biggest Europhobe there ever was. 'My best friend in the House of Commons is Ted Heath. It is funny, I resigned from his government over it. I always remember, he invited me into number 10's back garden. He was very nice. He said: "Now, Teddy. You have got to remember you are a very young man and you might be wrong." And I said: "Yes, I have thought about that very carefully, but I know I am right. I cannot vote to go into the Common Market. I think democracy is going to disappear and there will be mass unemployment." And we still both feel passionately about it. So we talk to each other and nobody gets bored.

The humour in *Hearts of Stone* cannot mask its cynicism towards Westminster. Written in 1968, four years into his 32-year career in Parliament, it is rooted in a period when he felt his colleagues treated him like a lesser form of pond life'. Despite this, its feel is Fifties rather than Sixties. Looking at him, you feel its author remains marooned there too, at least as far as appearances go. Hunched like a bald-headed eagle, he juts from his old-fashioned suit: a character from an Ealing comedy, an Alec Guinness or Alastair Sim.

He has invited us to his seaside home, a roomy place with the peeling features of a boarding house that has seen too many winters and too many guests. His sitting room too is decorated by flying ducks and paintings that look as if they have been completed by numbers. The door is propped ajar by a line of wooden chickens.

Taylor may be an adviser to the Association of Denture Prosthesis, but this is not the house of an MP on the make.

Taylor is so patently honest, it takes an effort to realise that many regard his politics — he is pro-hanging, and pro-birching, anti-abortion, etc — as extreme to the point of wickedness. He was too much even tor Mrs Thatcher, who in a rash moment in opposition, named him Shadow Scottish Secretary.

'I think I was the only person she ever assaulted,' he says. I was sitting next to Airey Neave and I brought up something about the abuses of the EEC, and she stretched out arid got my hand; like that [slap] and said: "Teddy, don't you mention the EEC again!"'

In the 1979 general election, as Tories all over the country were counting their majorities, Taylor lost Glasgow Cathcart. Although her influence got him shortlisted to fight the Southend East by-election the next year, Thatcher used the humiliation as an excuse to drop him from her team. (He says it was indicated there might be a job for him but only if he 'behaved' himself.) As it happens, it was his dignity in defeat - with Taylor praising his victorious opponent as a 'fine man' — that gave me the notion that he might be better than the 'Tartan Ayatollah' of Donald Dewar's put-down.

'Fine man' is a very Teddy Taylor phrase, part of a lexicon of civility last drawn from by Noel Coward for *Brief Encounter*. Most people are 'nice', although a few are 'nasty' or 'a bit strange' or 'unusual'. Things are 'horrible' or else 'lovely'. When he was an industrial relations officer for Clyde Shipbuilders in the late Fifties, for example, negotiating 'was really lovely because the unions were so nice'. One of the few people still to speak this way is the Prime Minister, who in his encomium to the late John Smith praised him for his lack of 'nastiness'. Both Major and Taylor hail from the struggling lower middle classes, who use soft words to cushion them from the hard times that lie just beyond. Just as Major-Ball's gnome business famously failed, Taylor's father, a stockbroker's clerk who took over the firm, went bankrupt. (He dropped dead in a phone box shortly afterwards.) Teddy's childhood was so disciplined and Presbyterian that it convinced him to give his own three children as much freedom as possible. He signed the pledge at the age of eight not out of religious fervour, but because the 'very nice chap at the church' gave a pound to every child who came forward. Nevertheless, he has stubbornly refused to touch alcohol since and he now considers it a bigger threat than drugs to the wellbeing of Southend, a fading resort of old ladies in big houses, visited only by the Threshers' delivery man. Taylor says his political awakening occurred on the tram to grammar school:, 'I used to travel through the Gorbals which was a bad housing area. I had great ideas about how I could improve things,' But why, I ask, Conservative ideas? No one with a social conscience (as Norman Tebbit never actually said) votes Tory.

'I often wonder why the heck I did join. Up at Glasgow University and later in my Parliamentary activities I've always found -- and it is a terrible thing for a Tory to say -- that Labour politicians tend to be the nicer blokes. They believe in something. But what struck me in Glasgow was that, although they were well-intentioned, they were acting against the interests of the working class. My first cause was to persuade my socialist friends that abolishing grammar schools and building council houses would undermine opportunities for the working class.'

Typically, once he had signed for the Tories, the main enemies he made were within his own party. There was, as he puts it, 'a bother' when he wrote an article for the university paper arguing that apartheid was a moral good. Taylor was thrown out, joined another debating society, and then stood for the council, first as a Progressive and as a Unionist. In 1959 he was elected at Cathcart and became its MP five years later. These early years in the Commons may have been lonely, but Taylor assiduously advocated causes guaranteed to make him lonelier still. He opposed David Steel's abortion Bill, voted against Rhodesian sanctions and spoke up for Enoch Powell when he was cut loose from the Shadow Cabinet and floated into the wilderness on a river of blood. Taylor got the reputation for overdoing it, in both senses. In 1969, he collapsed in the chamber with a suspected stroke. 'In my early twenties, a car door had banged me on the head and I had paralysis down my right side for four days. I had three attacks afterwards and in one of them I was taken to Westminster Hospital from the Commons. They thought I was dying. Ted Heath came and brought red roses.'

While recovering, Taylor met Sheila Duncan, a medical social worker, whom he had known as a child. He invited her and the matron to tea in the Commons and then asked Sheila to a concert at the Royal Albert Hall, to which he had free tickets. 'We clicked very much indeed and I invited her for a meal in the Commons.' This was not an expensive courtship. '... and I said; "I am a grizzly old bachelor but I think it would be a nice thing to get married, what do you feel?" And we got married very quickly and it has been a great success. I have honestly found, without being silly, that things always do work out for the best. I have a funny feeling if I had not ended up in hospital I would never have got married.' And not, I venture, had the joy of his three children, who, he says, have blossomed under his benevolent 'neglect'.

'But not just that. I think I was in danger of becoming a bit strange, a bit funny with my attitudes.' Politically?

'Yes, indeed. There are some things I feel very strongly about and there is always the danger of going over the top, as you know. Sheila will say: "The bad weather is not because of the EEC." The other thing is: it is all very well for me. I have never had responsibility, except briefly when I was a Minister in Ted Heath's government. There is a great danger thinking you have all the answers when you are sitting outside and the poor Ministers are rushed off their feet and having a miserable time. To a degree I think it can be sinful to say: "I know everything that is right and you are all mad."'

I suspect that part of this sense of sin comes not only from a righteous loathing of self-importance, but from a Calvinist terror of enjoyment. He describes being one of the eight whipless Tories last year as 'lovely'. 'We still have our weekly "cabinet" meetings every week and we change the "Prime Minister" every week,' he says and, yes, you can see the secret society, William and The Outlaws, fun in that. But what kicks are there in his other obsessions?

Take Libya, where he is convinced not only that Gadaffi was not behind Lockerbie, but that the bullet that killed PC Yvonne Fletcher in 1984 could not have come from the Libyan Embassy. However strong his case, defending a foreign regime predicated on 'just' terrorism not only sounds a little nutty but is a doomed campaign given the geopolitical reality that the West needs a scapegoat in the Middle East in order to rehabilitate Syria and the Lebanon.

Yet, at least this is a honourable lost cause. It is much harder to justify Taylor's years in the ultra right-wing Monday Club. Never mind justifying it: how could a lover of Bob Marley's music (he was introduced to it by his teenage daughter) and a champion of his

Asian constituents, stomach his fellow members?

'I Joined the Monday Club up in Scotland because I thought there was a need to stand up for the right-wing causes. But I resigned four years ago, basically because I felt they had got some unusual people in as members and I wasn't very happy. I felt they were getting out of control. I did go along and talk to a meeting the other week, the South East Essex Monday Club. A big dinner. I go every year."

And he doesn't hear racist remarks at these events?

'Well, they know if they try that with me they are going to get punished. It is something I feel passionate about. I hate this thing of anti-black, anti-Jewish, anti-Chinese. I think it is one of the foulest things. It is foul and it is filthy. If anyone tried that with me... I never think of myself as a violent person; but I think in that situation I would be.'

Then there are fruitcake hangers he associates with.

'Hanging is difficult,' he says, 'because of the people who support it. I do not like the letters I get: "Dear Mr Taylor, I agree with you on hanging. We should pull these rascals and vagabonds apart."'

But he remains in favour?

'Oh, very much. There is no doubt at all if you had capital punishment you would save a lot of innocent human lives. The evidence is overwhelming...'

But is it? And soon we are into an argument Taylor refuses to curtail. I try suing for peace several times because Jane Bown is getting worried there will be no time for pictures, but Taylor will accept only total surrender. At one stage, his dog enters, yapping in frenzied but hopeless pursuit of a fly. I hope this will distract Taylor, but the two obsessives, pet and owner, are entirely unaware of each other. Before we part, Taylor drives us, his reggae tapes blaring, through his constituency: past the football field he got dug, past the estate quartering Southend's 'poor single mothers' ('they get treated with so much contempt'), past the big houses where the elderly ladies are hitting the lunchtime sherry. He tells a great John Major story: 'He called me in and I bored him with my views on Europe. And when I had finished he said: "Can I tell you something in complete confidence? You mustn't repeat it. Privately, I think exactly as you do, I just disagree about the tactics." I was very impressed by this until I discovered that he says exactly the same thing to everyone who comes to see him.'

Hearts of Stone is a satire on such politicians. Compare Major with a man of real principle:

'Bob Marley was a fabulous chap,' Taylor says. 'He came from very humble origins and every week he held open house where people would queue up with their hard luck stories. One day he handed over £24,000. But the great thing was that he wasn't taken over by the establishment, although they kept trying. And his songs, you know, are just snippets of his thoughts. And his wee thoughts are lovely wee thoughts.'

The comparisons are left unmade, and we may question how lovely some of Taylor's wee thoughts would be if they were carried out. If only, you think, they always led him to company as rich as Marley's. Stepping onto the beach at Shoeburyness, where some of Southend's 10 per cent unemployed are asphyxiating themselves behind car windscreens, he says his only quarrel with his voters is that they don't care about politics.

Southend stayed away from his anti-Maastricht 'People's Rally' in droves, leaving the vacuum to be filled by what he euphemistically calls 'unusual people". In search of new allies, he addresses the Socialist Party in Lambeth Town Hall in September.

'I hope you realise,' he says when we shake hands, 'that I am of no significance whatsoever.' He is probably right and it may be just as well, but I feel sorry about it too. *Hearts of Stone* rule. Not OK.

Index

Printed in the United Kingdom by
Lightning Source UK Ltd., Milton Keynes
138337UK00001B/136/P